An Environmental Streamflow Assessment for the Santiam River Basin, Oregon

By John C. Risley, J. Rose Wallick, Joseph F. Mangano, and Krista L. Jones

Prepared in cooperation with the U.S. Army Corps of Engineers

Open-File Report 2012–1133

U.S. Department of the Interior
U.S. Geological Survey

U.S. Department of the Interior
KEN SALAZAR, Secretary

U.S. Geological Survey
Marcia K. McNutt, Director

U.S. Geological Survey, Reston, Virginia: 2012

For more information on the USGS—the Federal source for science about the Earth,
its natural and living resources, natural hazards, and the environment,
visit http://www.usgs.gov or call 1–888–ASK–USGS.

For an overview of USGS information products, including maps, imagery, and publications,
visit http://www.usgs.gov/pubprod

To order this and other USGS information products, visit http://store.usgs.gov

Suggested citation:
Risley, J.C., Wallick, J.R., Mangano, J.F., and Jones, K.F., 2012, An environmental streamflow assessment for the
Santiam River basin, Oregon: U.S. Geological Survey Open-File Report 2012-1133, 66 p.

Contents

Figures

Tables

Conversion Factors

Inch/Pound to SI

Multiply	By	To obtain
Length		
inch (in.)	25.4	millimeter (mm)
foot (ft)	0.3048	meter (m)
mile (mi)	1.609	kilometer (km)
Area		
square yard (yd^2)	0.08361	square meter (m^2)
square mile (mi^2)	2.590	square kilometer (km^2)
Volume		
cubic foot (ft^3)	0.02832	cubic meter (m^3)
acre-foot (acre-ft)	1,233	cubic meter (m^3)
Flow rate		
cubic foot per second (ft^3/s)	0.02832	cubic meter per second (m^3/s)
cubic foot per second per square mile [(ft^3/s)/mi^2]	0.01093	cubic meter per second per square kilometer [(m^3/s)/km^2]

Temperature in degrees Celsius (°C) may be converted to degrees Fahrenheit (°F) as follows:

$$°F = (1.8 × °C) + 32.$$

Temperature in degrees Fahrenheit (°F) may be converted to degrees Celsius (°C) as follows:

$$°C = (°F - 32)/1.8.$$

Vertical coordinate information is referenced to the North American Vertical Datum of 1988 (NAVD 88).

Horizontal coordinate information is referenced to the North American Datum of 1983 (NAD 83).

Elevation, as used in this report, refers to distance above the vertical datum.

An Environmental Streamflow Assessment for the Santiam River Basin, Oregon

By John C. Risley, J. Rose Wallick, Joseph F. Mangano, and Krista L. Jones

Abstract

The Santiam River is a tributary of the Willamette River in northwestern Oregon and drains an area of 1,810 square miles. The U.S. Army Corps of Engineers (USACE) operates four dams in the basin, which are used primarily for flood control, hydropower production, recreation, and water-quality improvement. The Detroit and Big Cliff Dams were constructed in 1953 on the North Santiam River. The Green Peter and Foster Dams were completed in 1967 on the South Santiam River. The impacts of the structures have included a decrease in the frequency and magnitude of floods and an increase in low flows. For three North Santiam River reaches, the median of annual 1-day maximum streamflows decreased 42–50 percent because of regulated streamflow conditions. Likewise, for three reaches in the South Santiam River basin, the median of annual 1-day maximum streamflows decreased 39–52 percent because of regulation.

In contrast to their effect on high flows, the dams increased low flows. The median of annual 7-day minimum flows in six of the seven study reaches increased under regulated streamflow conditions between 60 and 334 percent. On a seasonal basis, median monthly streamflows decreased from February to May and increased from September to January in all the reaches. However, the magnitude of these impacts usually decreased farther downstream from dams because of cumulative inflow from unregulated tributaries and groundwater entering the North, South, and main-stem Santiam Rivers below the dams. A Wilcox rank-sum test of monthly precipitation data from Salem, Oregon, and Waterloo, Oregon, found no significant difference between the pre- and post-dam periods, which suggests that the construction and operation of the dams since the 1950s and 1960s are a primary cause of alterations to the Santiam River basin streamflow regime.

In addition to the streamflow analysis, this report provides a geomorphic characterization of the Santiam River basin and the associated conceptual framework for assessing possible geomorphic and ecological changes in response to river-flow modifications. Suggestions for future biomonitoring and investigations are also provided. This study was one in a series of similar tributary streamflow and geomorphic studies conducted for the Willamette Sustainable Rivers Project. The Sustainable Rivers Project is a national effort by the USACE and The Nature Conservancy to develop environmental flow requirements in regulated river systems.

Introduction

In 2002, The Nature Conservancy (The Nature Conservancy) and the U.S. Army Corps of Engineers (USACE) formed the Sustainable Rivers Project (The Nature Conservancy, 2009), a partnership aimed at developing, implementing, and refining environmental flow requirements downstream from dams. Environmental flows can be defined as the streamflow needed to sustain ecosystems while continuing to meet human needs. Developing environmental flow requirements typically involves a collective process of stakeholders to identify and prioritize streamflow objectives. The process is a series of steps and feedback loops that include defining the streamflow requirements, implementing them into the dam operations, monitoring and modeling the streamflow changes and their effect on the river ecosystem, and then adjusting and refining the streamflow requirements if necessary. In addition to dams, other anthropogenic factors in a watershed can contribute to freshwater ecosystem degradation, such as water diversions, channel revetment, timber harvest, wetland draining, invasive species, gravel mining, and other factors, which also are commonly considered during the development process (Tharme, 2003; Acreman and Dunbar, 2004; Richter and others, 2006; The Nature Conservancy, 2009).

The Santiam River environmental flow study is a collaborative effort of the USACE, The Nature Conservancy, and the U.S. Geological Survey (USGS) to develop environmental flow requirements for the Santiam River, which is a tributary of the Willamette River in northwestern Oregon (fig. 1).

Scope of the Study

As a continuation of the Willamette Sustainable Rivers Project, the streamflow and geomorphic analyses from this study will assist the USACE and The Nature Conservancy in developing an environmental flow framework for the Santiam River basin. The framework will supplement a broader assemblage of ecological, hydrologic, and geomorphologic baseline data. The analyses include an assessment of changes to the ecosystem resulting from anthropogenic activities, such as dam operations and water withdrawals that have taken place in the basin.

The goals of this study are to analyze streamflow trends in the main reaches of the Santiam River basin and describe geomorphic and biological conditions to facilitate the development of environmental flow guidelines. Tasks to achieve these goals include:

1. Characterize streamflows in reaches under regulated and unregulated conditions.
2. Qualitatively describe dominant geomorphic and ecologic issues in reaches that could be affected by environmental flow modifications.
3. Communicate study results in a report and at future environmental flow workshops.

Purpose of the Report

This report will provide Santiam River basin stakeholders with a compilation of streamflow conditions under regulated and unregulated conditions in various reaches in the basin that are defined by their geomorphic and ecological characteristics. Using streamflow data and the results from the analysis of the data, it will be possible to identify the rate, frequency, duration, and timing of flow releases from Santiam River basin dams needed at downstream locations to achieve specific ecological and geomorphic objectives.

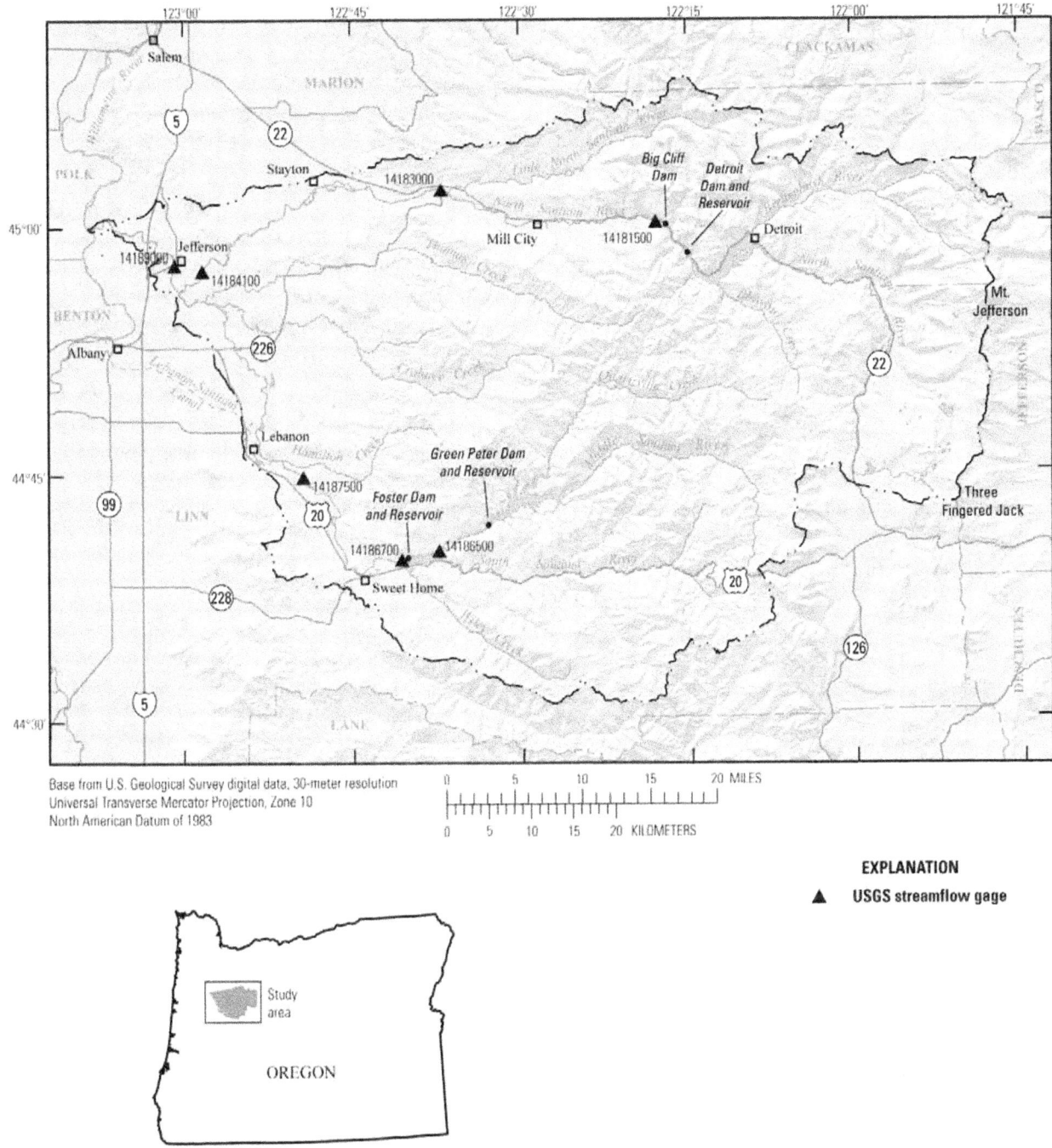

Figure 1. Map showing major streams and dams in the Santiam River basin, Oregon.

Description of the Study Area

The Santiam River basin is a subbasin of 1,810 mi^2 within the Willamette River basin in northwestern Oregon (fig. 1). Major tributaries in the Santiam River basin include the North Santiam River, Little North Santiam River, Middle Santiam River, South Santiam River, Thomas Creek, and Crabtree Creek. The North Santiam River begins high in the Cascade Range near Three Fingered Jack mountain and flows more than 100 mi before it joins the South Santiam River about 2 mi upstream from Jefferson. The South Santiam River begins at a lower elevation in the Western Cascades, west of the McKenzie River basin, and flows about 70 mi before joining the North Santiam River. From Jefferson, the main-stem Santiam River flows about 9 mi before it joins the Willamette River south of Salem and

north of Albany. Elevations in the basin range from 162 ft at the Willamette confluence to 10,497 ft at the summit of Mt. Jefferson. The river channel slope, within the study area downstream from the dams, ranges from less than 0.1 percent for the lower reach between the North and South Santiam River confluences to almost 1 percent for the North Santiam River below Big Cliff Dam (fig. 2). The basin has long, cool, wet winters and warm, dry summers. Average daily maximum and minimum temperatures at Stayton from 1951 to 2011 were 63 and 42°F, respectively. Average annual precipitation at Stayton for this period was 52.4 in. Because of greater precipitation at higher elevations, the mean annual precipitation for the entire Santiam River basin is 78.2 in. (1971–2000) (U.S. Geological Survey, 2012).

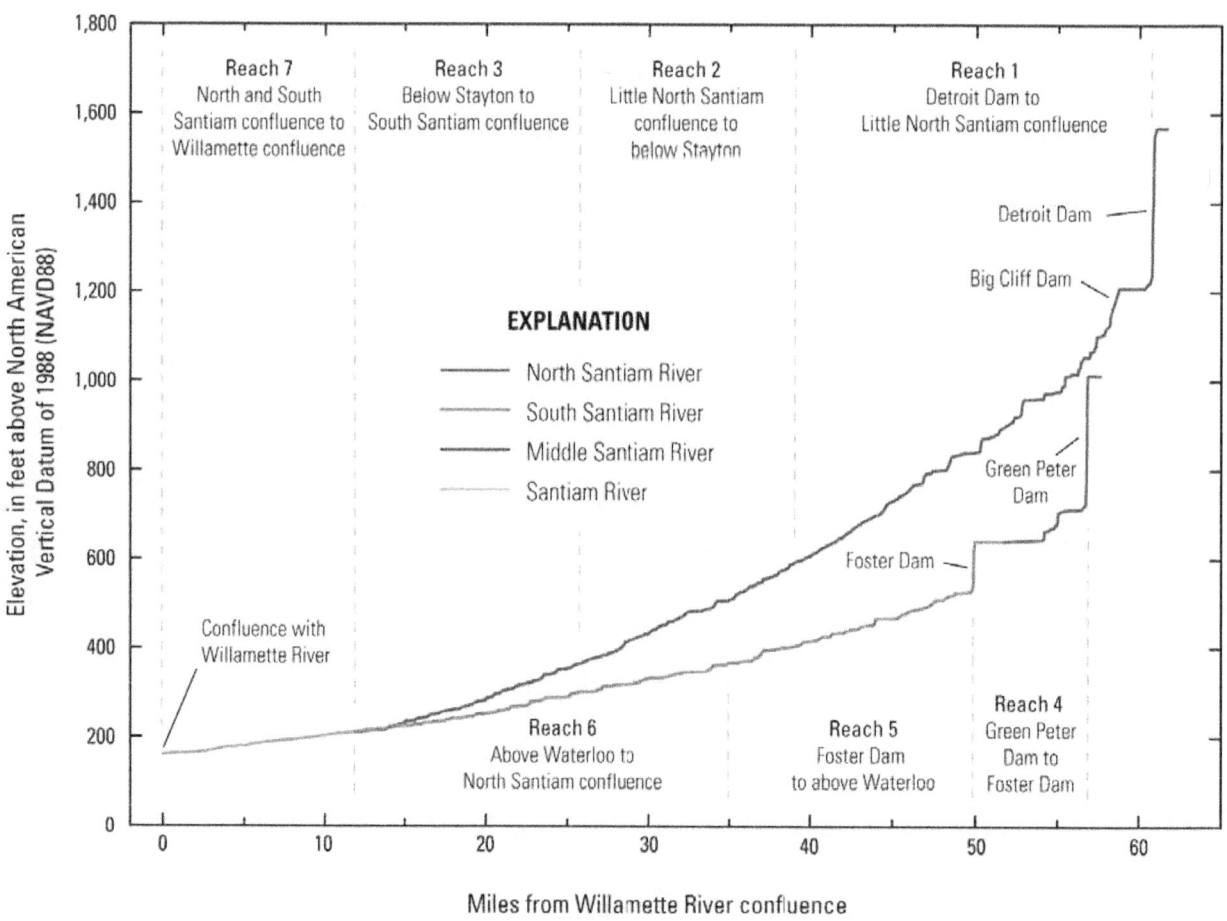

Figure 2. Diagram showing profile of the Santiam River basin, Oregon.

Higher elevation areas are underlain by young, relatively permeable material consisting of High Cascade volcanic rocks and glacial deposits. Middle and lower elevations of the basin contain the older, less permeable, weathered volcanic material of the Western Cascades. The lower reach of the river, near the Willamette River confluence, mainly comprises a wide, unconstrained flood plain underlain by Quaternary alluvium (fig. 3). The economy of the Santiam River basin is supported by agriculture, timber harvesting, recreation, and manufacturing. Approximately 70 percent of the basin is forested. Timber is harvested on both private and Federal lands. Higher elevation areas in the basin are managed by the Willamette National Forest.

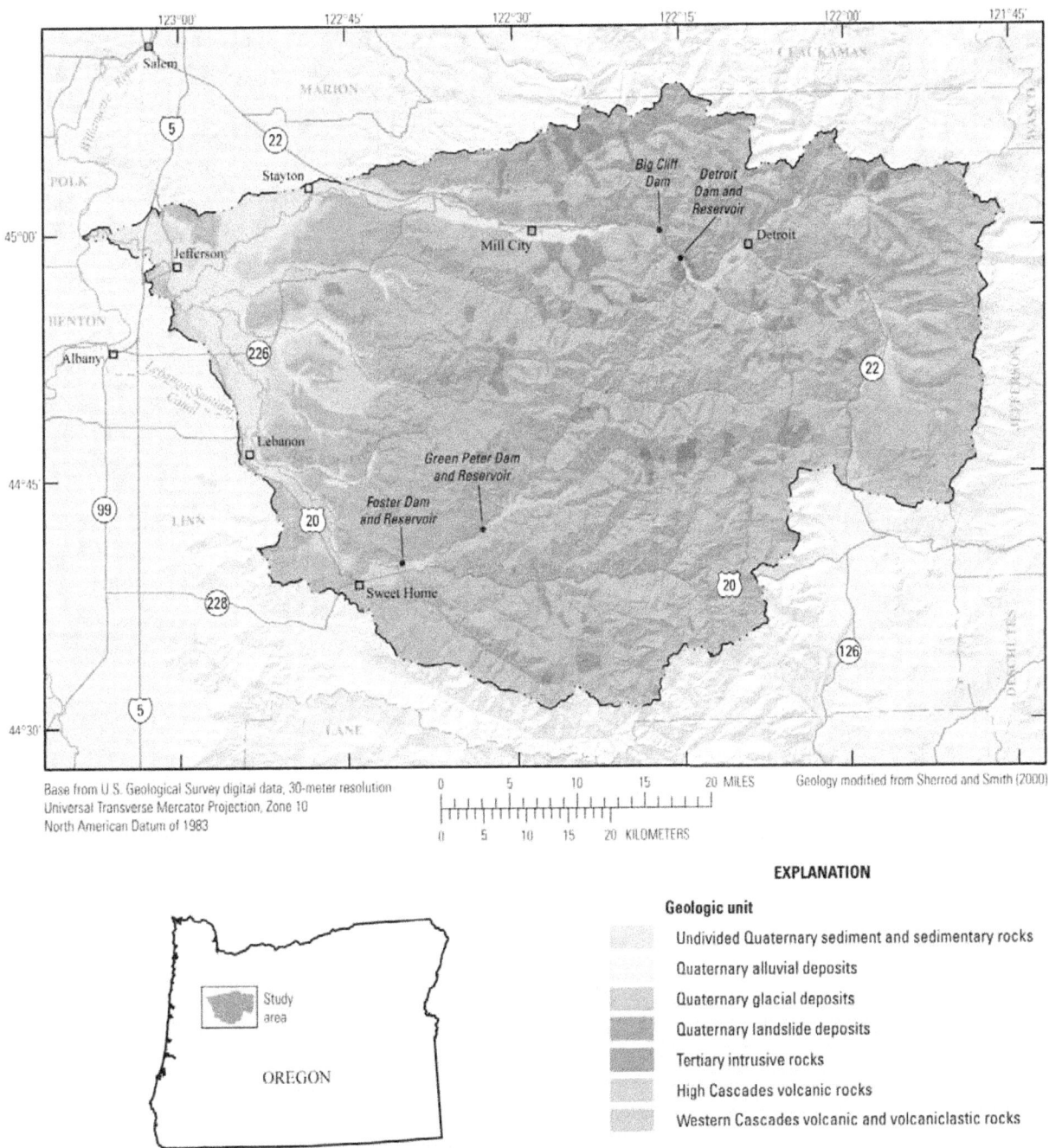

Base from U.S. Geological Survey digital data, 30-meter resolution
Universal Transverse Mercator Projection, Zone 10
North American Datum of 1983

Geology modified from Sherrod and Smith (2000)

EXPLANATION

Geologic unit

Undivided Quaternary sediment and sedimentary rocks

Quaternary alluvial deposits

Quaternary glacial deposits

Quaternary landslide deposits

Tertiary intrusive rocks

High Cascades volcanic rocks

Western Cascades volcanic and volcaniclastic rocks

Figure 3. Map showing geology of the Santiam River basin, Oregon.

Study Framework

The Santiam River system in the study area was divided into seven reaches, each having distinct streamflow, geomorphic, and ecological conditions (fig. 4, table 1). The North Santiam River portion of the study area was divided into three reaches. Reach 1 extends from Detroit Dam to the confluence of the Little North Santiam River. Reach 2 continues downstream to river mile (RM) 26 near Stayton. Reach 3 continues downstream to the South Santiam River confluence. The South Santiam River basin was also divided into three reaches. Reach 4 is along the Middle Santiam River, a tributary of the South Santiam River, between Green Peter Dam and Foster Lake reservoir. Reaches 5 and 6 extend from Foster Dam to RM 23.4 (upstream from USGS streamflow gaging station (hereinafter "gage") at Waterloo [14187500]) and from RM 23.4 to the North Santiam River confluence, respectively. The final reach, Reach 7, extends from confluence of the North and South Santiam Rivers through Jefferson to the Willamette River confluence. For all reaches where the downstream boundary is near a major stream confluence, the downstream boundary was set just upstream from the confluence. Streamflow from the confluent stream is included in the streamflow of the next downstream reach. This was done to minimize the difference in streamflow between both ends of the reach and to use a single representative reach discharge in the analyses.

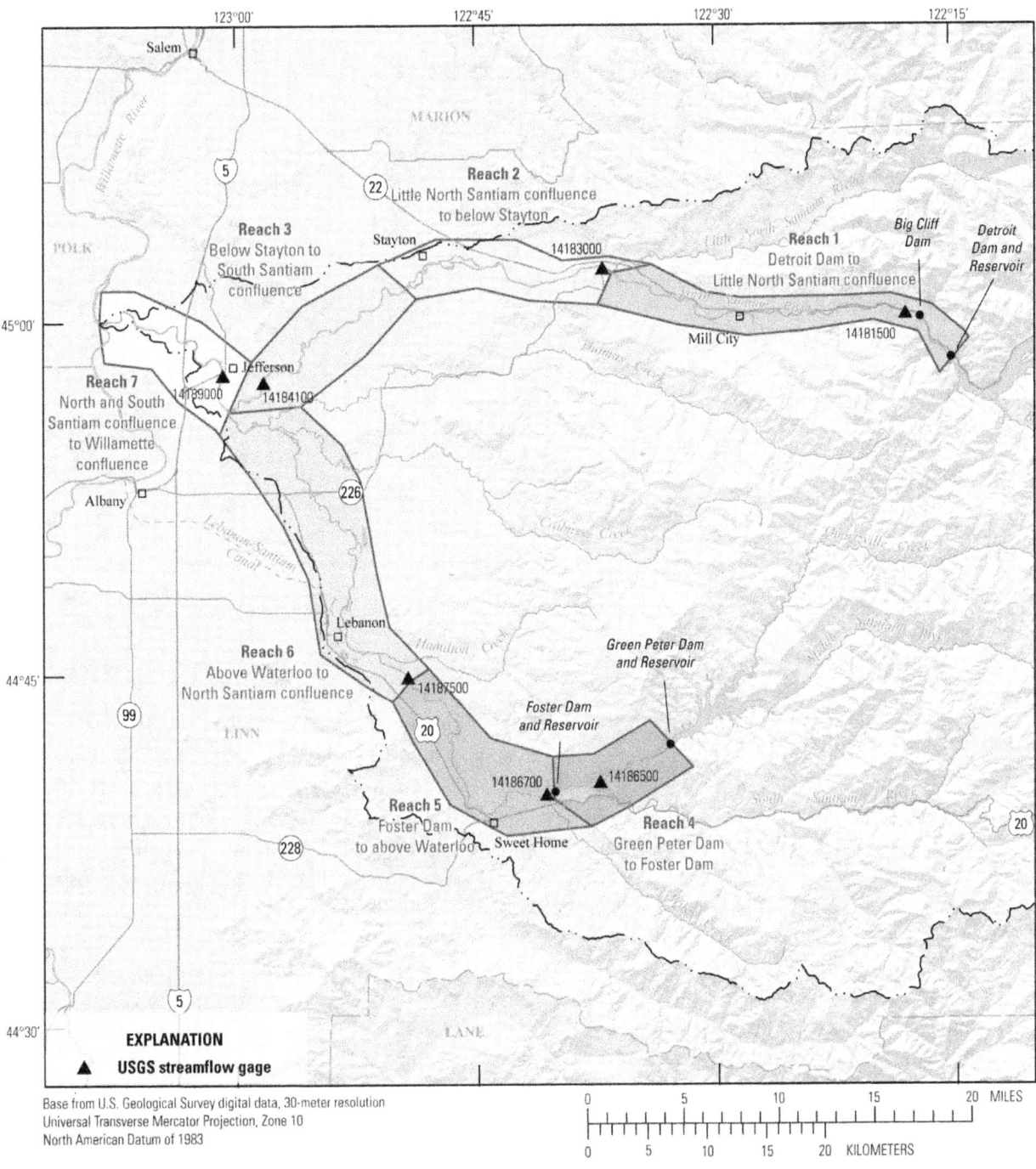

Figure 4. Map showing location of study reaches, Santiam River basin, Oregon.

Table 1. Study reach locations in the Santiam River basin, Oregon.

Reach number	River name	Upstream end description	Upstream end river mile	Downstream end description	Reach length (miles)
		Northern basin			
1	North Santiam	Detroit Dam	60.9	Little North Santiam River confluence	21.7
2	North Santiam	Little North Santiam River confluence	39.2	Below Stayton, Oregon	13.2
3	North Santiam	Below Stayton, Oregon	26.0	South Santiam confluence	14.2
		Southern basin			
4	Middle Santiam	Green Peter Dam	5.5	Foster Dam	5.5
5	South Santiam	Foster Dam	38.1	Above Waterloo, Oregon	14.7
6	South Santiam	Above Waterloo, Oregon	23.4	N. Santiam River confluence	23.4
		Lower basin			
7	Lower Santiam	North and South Santiam River confluence	11.8	Willamette confluence	11.8

Streamflow Regulation

The USACE operates four dams in the Santiam River basin (fig. 5, table 2). The Detroit and the Big Cliff Dams, on the North Santiam River, were completed in 1953. In addition to flood control and recreation uses, the Detroit Dam also produces up to 100 megawatts of power. The smaller Big Cliff Dam, 3 mi downstream from the Detroit Dam, is also used for hydropower production and for regulating power-generating water releases from Detroit Dam. The Green Peter and Foster Dams, in the South Santiam River basin, were completed in 1968. The two dams work in conjunction to provide flood control, hydropower production, irrigation supply, recreation, water-quality improvement, and aquatic habitat. Foster Dam, about 7 mi downstream from Green Peter Dam, is used to produce hydropower and regulate power-generating water releases from Green Peter Dam. The Green Peter and Foster Dams have generators capable of producing a combined total of 100 megawatts. Surface-water withdrawals for urban water supply and irrigation are made at locations downstream from the dams. The city of Salem withdraws approximately 67 ft^3/s from the North Santiam River at RM 31.0 on Geren Island (Oregon Water Resources Department, 2012). On the South Santiam River, an average of 90 ft^3/s of streamflow (water years 1993–2011) was diverted mostly for municipal water supply to the Lebanon-Santiam Canal at RM 20.8 as measured at the USGS gage on the canal (14187600).

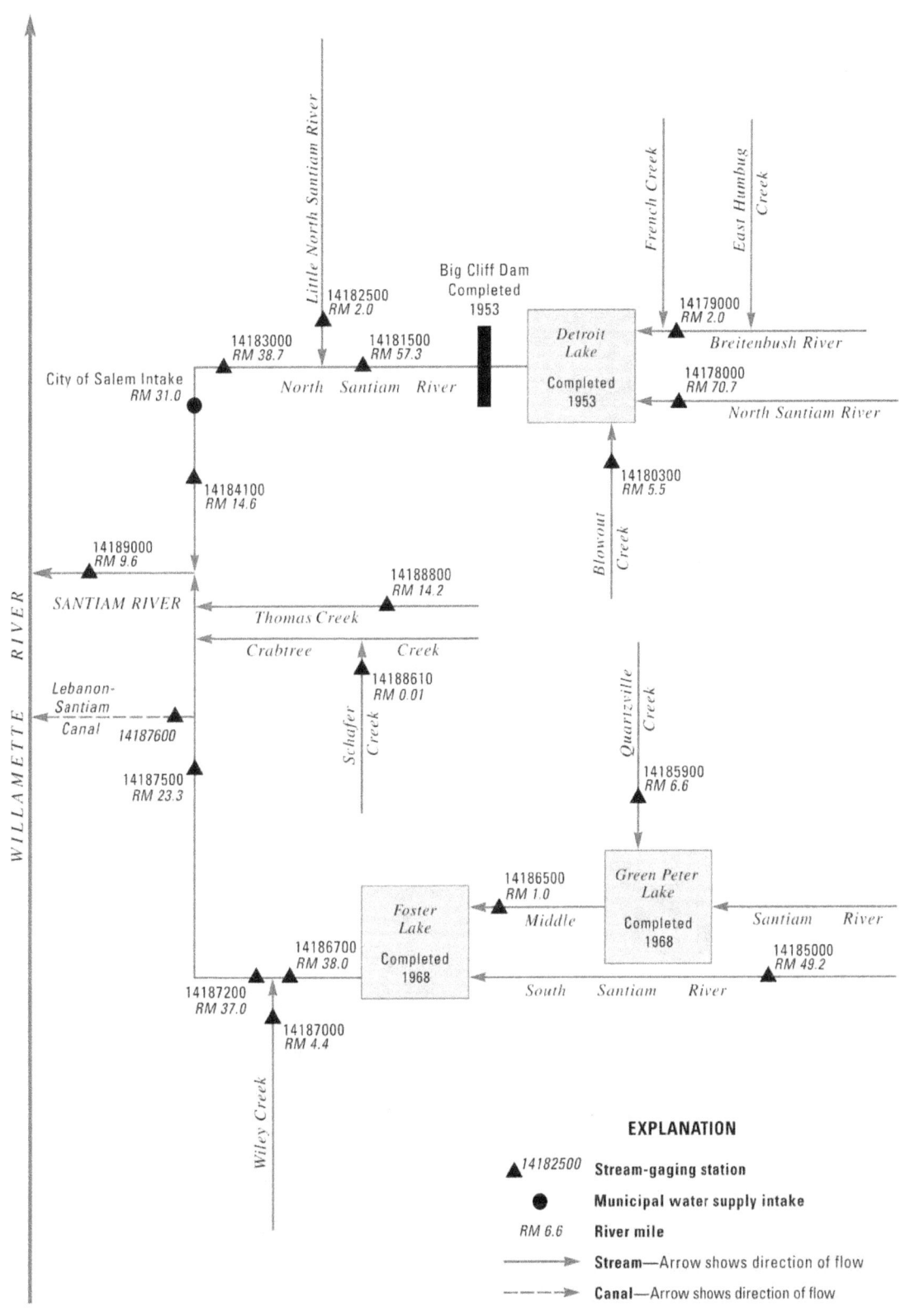

Figure 5. Diagram showing dams and selected streamflow gaging stations in the Santiam River basin, Oregon.

Table 2. Dams in the Santiam River Basin, Oregon.

[Data from the U.S. Army Corps of Engineers, http://www.nwd-wc.usace.army.mil/report/, accessed October 27, 2011. Abbreviations: fad, feet above North American Vertical Datum of 1988; na, not applicable; mi², square miles; KW, kilowatt; HP, hydropower; FC, flood control; N, navigation; I, irrigation; F, fisheries; WQ, water-quality; RR, Reregulation; R, recreation.]

| Dam name | River | Year completed | Lake pool elevation | | Upstream drainage area (mi²) | River mile | Reservoir useable storage (acre-feet) | Reservoir surface area (acres) | Reservoir use | Maximum power output (KW) |
			Min. (fad)	Max. (fad)						
Detroit	North Santiam	1953	1,450	1,574	435	60.9	321,000	3,500	FC, HP, N, F, I, WQ, R	100,000
Big Cliff	North Santiam	1953	1,180	1,210	449	58.1	na	na	RR, HP, R	18,000
Green Peter	Middle Santiam	1968	922	1,015	276	5.5	312,500	3,720	FC, HP, N, I, F, WQ, R	80,000
Foster	South Santiam	1968	613	641	492	38.1	28,300	1,220	RR, FC, HP, N, I, F, WQ, R	20,000

Previous Santiam River basin Studies

Speers and Versteeg (1982) presented procedures for long-term forecasts of spring-season water supply for Detroit reservoir operations. Laenen and Risley (1997) and Lee and Risley (2002) created a set of precipitation-runoff watershed models for the entire Willamette River basin for water-quality and ground-water analyses, respectively. In these studies, the Santiam River basin was divided into 22 subbasins, from which 22 watershed models were created. Thayer (1936a, 1936b) presented early research on geology in the Santiam River basin. Helm and Leonard (1977) described groundwater resources in the lower basin. Conlon and others (2005) described groundwater hydrologic conditions in the entire Willamette River basin, including the Santiam River basin. Fletcher and Davidson (1988) analyzed the geomorphic response to regulation and bank protection in the lower section of the South Santiam River. Hill and Priest (1992) described the geologic setting of the Santiam Pass area. Sherrod and others (1996) presented an overview of geology, hydrology, and geothermal resources in the North Santiam River basin.

The USGS conducted studies pertaining to the effect of reservoir operations in the Santiam River basin on water temperatures in and downstream from reservoirs. Laenen and Hanson (1985) and Hanson and Crumrine (1991) simulated water temperatures downstream from reservoirs on the North and South Santiam Rivers using a daily mean, one-dimensional Lagrangian computer model. More recent studies by Sullivan and Rounds (2004), Sullivan and others (2007), and Buccola and Rounds (2011) also simulated water temperatures on the North Santiam River in and downstream from reservoirs using temporally and spatially detailed two-dimensional models. In addition to water temperatures, heavy flooding and landslides in the late 1990s resulted in a major water-quality concern over suspended sediment in North Santiam River. Uhrich and Bragg (2003) presented a method for estimating suspended-sediment loads and yields using turbidity data. Bragg and Uhrich (2010) presented a suspended-sediment budget for the entire North Santiam River basin. Suspended sediment and turbidity in the basin are also described in Bragg and others (2007), Piatt and others (2011), and Sobieszcyk and others (2007).

Environmental Regulatory Issues

In early 1999, the National Marine Fisheries Service (NMFS) listed Upper Willamette River Chinook salmon (*Oncorhynchus tshawytscha*) and the Upper Willamette River steelhead (*Oncorhynchus mykiss*) in the Santiam River basin and other upper Willamette River basins as threatened under the Federal Endangered Species Act (ESA). In 1993, the U.S. Fish and Wildlife Service (USFWS) listed the Oregon chub (*Oregonichthys crameri*) as endangered in Marion and Linn Counties, which includes the Santiam River basin. In 2010, the Oregon chub was reclassified from endangered to threatened. As a result of these listings, the USACE submitted its first Biological Assessment in 2000 and a supplemental Biological Assessment in 2007 for the Willamette River basin that included specific recovery plans for the Santiam River basin (U.S. Army Corps of Engineers, 2000, 2007).

In July 2008, NMFS released their decision on the Biological Assessment plans through a Willamette Project Biological Opinion (National Marine Fisheries Service, 2008a; 2008b). The USFWS also released a Biological Opinion for the Willamette River basin because they have jurisdiction over the Oregon chub (U.S. Fish and Wildlife Service, 2008). NMFS and the USFWS decided that the USACE Biological Assessment plans were insufficient for mitigating the effect of the water projects on critical habitat. The Biological Opinion ordered additional measures, which included improved fish passage, temperature control, and changes in downstream streamflows. The Biological Opinion includes flow-release targets for Big Cliff and Foster Dams for different seasonal life histories for the ESA-listed fish (table 3). The Biological Opinion also includes a measure for implementing environmental flow releases from the dams.

Table 3. Minimum and maximum streamflow objectives below Big Cliff and Foster Dams.
[Source: National Marine Fisheries Service, 2008]

Period	Primary Use	Minimum flow (ft^3/s)	Maximum flow (ft^3/s)
Big Cliff Dam			
September 1–October 15	Chinook spawning	1,500	3,000
October 16–January 31	Chinook incubation	1,200	
February 1–March 15	Chinook rearing/adult migration	1,000	
March 16–May 31	steelhead spawning	1,500	3,000
June 1–July 15	steelhead incubation	1,200	
July 16–August 31	steelhead rearing	1,000	
Foster Dam			
September 1–October 15	Chinook spawning	1,500	3,000
October 16–January 31	Chinook incubation	1,100	
February 1–March 15	Chinook rearing	800	
March 16–May 15	steelhead spawning	1,500	3,000
May 16–June 30	steelhead incubation	1,100	
July 1–August 31	steelhead rearing	800	

The Oregon Department of Environmental Quality (ODEQ), as required under the Federal Clean Water Act, released a stream-temperature Total Maximum Daily Load (TMDL) plan in 2006 for the Willamette River basin (Oregon Department of Environmental Quality, 2006). Stream reaches in the North and South Santiam River basins found to be thermally impaired and not meeting state temperature standards for salmonid rearing, spawning, and cold-water refuges, as a result of reservoir releases, channel geomorphology alterations, streamflow diversions, and limited riparian shade, were placed on the Federal Clean Water Act section 303(d) list as having exceeded their temperature TMDL.

Methods

For this study, various methods were employed to assess the effects of dams and withdrawals on streamflows. These included a compilation of measured and estimated daily mean gage statistics under regulated and unregulated conditions, bankfull streamflow estimation, pre- and post-dam peak-flow analysis, and a pre- and post-dam period climate comparison.

Streamflow Data

Measured and Estimated Streamflow

The USGS began continuous streamflow monitoring within the Santiam River basin (table 4) in the 1920s. Eighteen of these stations were active during water year 2011. The stations with the longest streamflow time series are the North Santiam River at Mehama (14183000: 1921–2011) and the South Santiam River at Waterloo (14187500: 1923–2011). From 2005 to 2010, the USGS also operated eight temporary streamflow measurement sites (14183430, 14183450, 14183500, 14183550, 14183570, 14183580, 14183585, and 14183590) in the vicinity of Geren Island on the North Santiam River. (Map at *http://or.water.usgs.gov/northsantiam/sites/*). Streamflow and stage were measured intermittently at these sites during six summers to create rating curves. One station was upstream from Geren Island, five stations were in the north and south channels around the island, and two stations were in side diversion cannels. The purpose of the data monitoring was to gain a better understanding of the spatial and temporal distribution of surface waters during low-flow conditions upstream and downstream from the island, in the alcoves and secondary channels, and near the Salem municipal water-supply intakes.

Seven of the gages from table 4 were representative of flow conditions in the seven defined study reaches and could be used in the statistical analyses (table 5). Streamflow data for Reaches 1, 2, 6, and 7 represented unregulated and regulated flow conditions because they extended from the 1920s and 1930s to water year 2011. However, for the other three reaches (Reaches 3, 4, and 5), it was necessary to augment the measured streamflow period with computed regulated and computed unregulated daily mean streamflow time series provided by the USACE. Microsoft® Excel® files containing measured and estimated daily mean streamflows for the seven reaches can be downloaded from the link in Appendix A.

Table 4. U.S. Geological Survey streamflow gaging stations in the Santiam River basin, Oregon

[A water year is from October 1 of the previous year to September 30. Abbreviations: mi^2, square miles; *, stage or elevation data only; na, not applicable.]

Station number	Streamflow station name	Drainage area (mi^2)	Period of record (water years)
14178000	North Santiam River below Boulder Creek near Detroit, Oregon	216	1928–2011
14178700	East Humbug Creek near Detroit, Oregon	7.32	1978–1994
14179000	Breitenbush River above French Creek near Detroit, Oregon	108	1932–1987; 1998–2011
14179100	French Creek near Detroit, Oregon	9.9	2002–2005
14180300	Blowout Creek near Detroit, Oregon	26.0	1998–2011
14180500	Detroit Lake near Detroit, Oregon	437	1953–2004*
14181500	North Santiam River at Niagara, Oregon	453	1938–2011
14181750	Rock Creek near Mill City, Oregon	14.8	2005–2008
14182400	Little North Santiam River below Canyon Creek near Mehama, Oregon	93.0	2007–2008
14182500	Little North Santiam River near Mehama, Oregon	112	1931–2011
14183000	North Santiam River at Mehama, Oregon	654	1921–2011
14184100	North Santiam River at Greens Bridge near Jefferson, Oregon	736	1964–1967; 2011
14185000	South Santiam River below Cascadia, Oregon	174	1935–2011
14185700	Middle Santiam River near Upper Soda, Oregon	74.6	1981–1994
14185800	Middle Santiam River near Cascadia, Oregon	104	1964–1981; 1988
14185880	Packers Gulch near Cascadia, Oregon	7.45	1983–1986
14185900	Quartzville Creek near Cascadia, Oregon	99.2	1963–2011
14186000	Middle Santiam River near Foster, Oregon	271	1931–1947
14186100	Green Peter Lake near Foster, Oregon	273	1974–2003*
14186200	Middle Santiam River below Green Peter Lake near Foster, Oregon	273	2010–2011*
14186500	Middle Santiam River at mouth near Foster, Oregon	287	1950–1966
14186600	Foster Lake at Foster, Oregon	492	1974–2003*
14186700	South Santiam River at Foster, Oregon	493	1966–1973
14187000	Wiley Creek near Foster, Oregon	51.8	1947–1973; 1988–2011
14187100	Wiley Creek at Foster, Oregon	62.3	1973–1988
14187200	South Santiam River near Foster, Oregon	557	1973–2011
14187500	South Santiam River at Waterloo, Oregon	640	1923–2011

Table 4. U.S. Geological Survey streamflow gaging stations in the Santiam River basin, Oregon.—continued

[A water year is from October 1 of the previous year to September 30. Abbreviations: mi^2, square miles; *, stage or elevation data only; na, not applicable.]

Station number	Streamflow station name	Drainage area (mi^2)	Period of record (water years)
14187600	Lebanon Santiam Canal near Lebanon, Oregon	na	1993–2011
14188000	Albany Santiam Canal near Lebanon, Oregon	na	1926–1957
14188610	Schafer Creek near Lacomb, Oregon	1.03	1993–2011
14188700	Crabtree Creek near Crabtree, Oregon	111	1963–1970
14188800	Thomas Creek near Scio, Oregon	110	1962–1987; 2002–2011
14188850	Thomas Creek near Crabtree, Oregon	143	2002–2008*
14189000	Santiam River at Jefferson, Oregon	1,790	1940–2011

Computed Unregulated Streamflow

The USACE compiled and computed unregulated daily mean streamflow time series for water years 1936–2009 at North Santiam River at Detroit Dam (upstream from 14181500), North Santiam River at Mehama (14183000), Middle Santiam River at Green Peter Dam (upstream from 14186500), South Santiam River at Foster Dam (14186700), South Santiam River at Waterloo (14187500), and Santiam River at Jefferson (14189000) (Alan Donner, U.S. Army Corps of Engineers, written commun., 2011). These time series are an estimate of streamflow (1936–2009) at these locations if the four USACE dams had not been constructed. For this study, these time series were used to evaluate the hydrologic effect of the dams by comparing pre- and post-dam streamflow conditions.

The daily mean streamflow time series for the North Santiam River at Detroit Dam and the Middle Santiam River at Green Peter Dam were computed using USACE reservoir models. However, the time series for the other locations were computed by adding these simulated time series with estimated downstream local inflows. The inflow time series were computed using correlations with nearby unregulated USGS streamflow records in the region. Details on how the unregu-

lated time series were computed are provided in Appendix B.

For Reaches 1, 3, and 4, it was necessary to adjust the USACE unregulated daily mean streamflows using a drainage-area ratio to create unregulated streamflow conditions at the USGS gages in those reaches. Details of the adjustments are included in the Excel files for each reach (Appendix A).

Computed Regulated Streamflow

USACE also provided this study with computed regulated daily mean streamflow time series for Big Cliff Dam (1960–2011), Green Peter Dam (1967–2011), and Foster Dam (1968–2011). The time series for Green Peter and Foster Dams were used to create the Reach 4 and 5 regulated streamflow time series, respectively, because measured USGS streamflow data were unavailable at these locations for these time periods.

Bankfull Discharge Estimation Methods

In geomorphology, bankfull discharge is generally assumed to represent the geomorphically significant flow that fills the banks without spilling onto the flood plain. It is commonly used as a streamflow metric in environmental flow studies when creating flow prescriptions that will meet the habitat needs of an aquatic or terrestrial species at various life stages. The estimation of bankfull discharge has substantial uncertainty because it has to be estimated at a specific location and is not necessarily representative of a reach. Wolman and Miller (1960) defined bankfull discharge as having a recurrence interval of 1.5 years in a variety of rivers. However, that approach could not be used consistently in all seven study reaches, because not all the reaches have an adequate number of years of pre-dam peak-flow data to complete a flood-frequency analysis.

For this study, several methods of estimating bankfull discharge were compared and evaluated. These included bankfull-discharge estimates provided by the USACE, unit-discharge estimates based on USACE estimates, field observations at gages, calculation of the 1.5-year peak-flow frequency, and channel cross-section plots derived from high-flow measurement data

(table 5). Estimates based on the latter method are not included in the table because of insufficient channel detail in the data or because flow events had insufficient magnitude.

Bankfull flood stage and discharge estimates for gages in Reaches 2, 6, and 7 were previously determined by the USACE using field-site-level surveys, aerial photography, and flood analyses (Keith Duffy, U.S. Army Corps of Engineers, written commun., 2011). The corresponding gages, which include North Santiam River at Mehama, Oregon (14183000) (Reach 2), South Santiam River at Waterloo, Oregon (14187500) (Reach 6), and Santiam River at Jefferson, Oregon (14189000) (Reach 7), have the longest streamflow records in the Santiam River basin and also are used as flood-forecast sites by the U.S. National Weather Service River Forecasting Center.

Table 5. Study-reach streamflow gaging stations and bankfull discharge and flood estimates, Santiam River basin, Oregon.

[Abbreviation: USACE, U.S. Army Corps of Engineers; LPIII, Log Pearson III flood frequency analysis; mi², square mile; ft³/s, cubic feet per second; na, not available. River mile is distance from the nearest downstream confluence.]

Reach number	Station number	Streamflow gaging-station name	Drainage area (mi²)	River mile	Bank full discharge estimates				LPIII flood frequency		USACE flood estimate (ft³/s)
					USACE (ft³/s)	Unit discharge estimate (ft³/s)	USGS field estimate (ft³/s)	Pre-dam period of record	1.5-year peak (ft³/s)		
1	14181500	North Santiam River at Niagara, Oregon	453	57.3	na	11,100	3,000	1909–52	16,700		na
2	14183000	North Santiam River at Mehama, Oregon	654	38.7	17,000	na	na	1906–52	28,500		30,500
3	14184100	North Santiam River at Greens Bridge near Jefferson, Oregon	732	14.6	na	18,000	na	na	na		na
4	14186500	Middle Santiam River at mouth near Foster, Oregon	287	1.0	na	7,050	na	1950–66	23,100		na
5	14186700	South Santiam River at Foster, Oregon	493	38.0	na	12,100	5,550	na	na		na
6	14187500	South Santiam River at Waterloo, Oregon	640	23.3	18,000	na	na	1906–52	31,500		25,700
7	14189000	Santiam River at Jefferson, Oregon	1,790	9.6	35,000	na	na	1908–52	62,400		55,900

For gages in the other study reaches, Reach 1 (14181500), Reach 3 (14184100), Reach 4 (14186500), and Reach 5 (14186700), bankfull discharge was estimated using an average of the unit discharges of the three USACE estimates for Reaches 2, 6, and 7. The unit discharges were computed by dividing the USACE estimates by the upstream drainage areas of the gages. The average of the three unit discharges was 24.6 $(ft^3/s)/mi^2$. This value was multiplied by the upstream drainage areas of the Reach 1, Reach 3, Reach 4, and Reach 5 gages to get bankfull discharge estimates for those reaches.

Field estimates of bankfull stage were made by the USGS for this study in January 2011 at the gages for Reach 1, North Santiam River at Niagara, Oregon (14181500), and for Reach 5, South Santiam River at Foster, Oregon (14186700). Stage height was estimated using a hand-held leveler because time and funding restrictions precluded measuring stage heights using a transit and rod. At both gages, readings from outside staff gages were taken while standing just below flood-plain level. The height of the observer was then subtracted from the staff reading. With a bankfull stage estimate, the bankfull discharge could be determined using the rating curve. In comparison to the other two methods of bankfull discharge estimation, these field observation estimates were considerably smaller.

A major limitation with bankfull discharge estimates made from field observation is that their representation of the reach is limited to proximity of the gage. It was not possible to make a bankfull discharge field estimate at the Reach 3 gage, South Santiam River at Green's Bridge near Jefferson (14184100), because of visual obstructions in the line of sight. It was also not possible to make a bankfull discharge field estimate at the Reach 4 gage, Middle Santiam River at mouth near Foster (14186500) because it was active only during the pre-dam period (1950–66) and is now submerged beneath Foster Reservoir. Field estimates were not made at gages for Reach 2, North Santiam River at Mehama (14183000), Reach 6, South Santiam River at

Waterloo (14187500), or Reach 7, Santiam River at Jefferson (14189000) because the USACE had previously estimated bankfull discharge at those sites.

Using measured pre-dam annual peak-flow data, the 1.5-year flood frequency, based on the Bulletin 17B Log Pearson III method (Interagency Committee on Water Data, 1982), was computed for the gages in Reaches 1, 2, 6, and 7. It was not possible to compute a flood frequency for the Reach 3 and Reach 5 gages, 14184100 and 14186700, respectively, because their records did not contain peak-flow data during the pre-dam period. As shown in table 5, the 1.5-year flood frequencies were higher than the other USACE bankfull discharge estimates for the Reach 2 (14183000), Reach 6 (14187500), and Reach 7 (14189000) gages.

To estimate bankfull discharge from channel cross-section plots, it is sometimes possible to create the plots using stage and discharge data from USGS discharge measurement notes from gages. With a detailed channel cross section during a measured high-flow event, bank and flood-plain features can sometimes be defined to estimate the bankfull stage. With a bankfull stage estimate, the bankfull discharge can be determined from the rating curve. The bankfull stage estimate could not be estimated at the Reach 1 gage on the North Santiam River at Niagara (14181500) and the Reach 4 gage at the Middle Santiam River at the mouth near Foster (1418650) because the channel cross-section plots from these high-flow events contained insufficient detail to delineate the streambank and flood-plain features. Bankfull stage estimates for Reach 3 gage on the North Santiam River at Green's Bridge near Jefferson (14184200) and the Reach 5 gage on the South Santiam River at Foster (14186700) were not made because the magnitude of high-flow measurements was insufficient.

Indicators of Hydrologic Alteration

Developed by The Nature Conservancy for the Sustainable Rivers Project, the Indicators of Hydrologic Alteration (IHA) software program allows users to compute streamflow statistics that can be used to quantify hydrologic changes resulting from the construction of dams and diversion canals in a river basin (The Nature Conservancy, 2007). For a given daily mean streamflow record, the program computes an extreme low-flow threshold, high-flow threshold, small floods (2-year events), and large floods (10-year events) (table 6). The high-flow threshold, which is also the 25 percent streamflow exceedance, is analogous to a high-flow pulse. The extreme low-flow category includes the lowest 10 percent of daily mean streamflows that are less than the high-flow threshold. The IHA program estimates flood magnitudes for the 2- and 10-year recurrence intervals using a Weibull distribution.

Streamflow statistics in table 6 were computed using data provided by the USACE representing unregulated streamflow conditions for each reach. A common period (water years 1953–2009) was used for all seven reaches. Like bankfull flow estimates, estimates of low flows, pulse flows, small floods, and large floods are used in environmental flow studies to define flow prescriptions that will meet the habitat needs of an aquatic or terrestrial species at various life stages. Output from the IHA program can be downloaded at the link in Appendix C.

Table 6. Indicators of Hydrologic Alteration streamflow statistics at study reach streamflow gaging stations based on unregulated streamflow conditions in the Santiam River basin, Oregon, for water years 1953–2009.

[Abbreviation: ft^3/s, cubic feet per second.]

Reach number	Station number	Streamflow gaging station name	Extreme low-flow threshold (ft^3/s)	High-flow threshold (ft^3/s)	2-year flood (ft^3/s)	10-year flood (ft^3/s)
1	14181500	North Santiam River at Niagara, Oregon	635	2,810	21,300	32,200
2	14183000	North Santiam River at Mehama, Oregon	685	4,270	35,400	53,900
3	14184100	North Santiam River at Greens Bridge near Jefferson, Oregon	767	4,780	39,600	60,400
4	14186500	Middle Santiam River at mouth near Foster, Oregon	130	2,190	20,700	33,200
5	14186700	South Santiam River at Foster, Oregon	210	3,420	32,600	49,900
6	14187500	South Santiam River at Waterloo, Oregon	223	3,980	35,800	59,100
7	14189000	Santiam River at Jefferson, Oregon	551	10,100	85,000	144,000

Water-Use Compilation

Major surface-water withdrawals along the lower reaches of the North Santiam, South Santiam, and Santiam Rivers were compiled in order to quantify natural streamflow conditions. Much of the water-use data and information was from the Oregon Water Resources Department website (*http://www.wrd.state.or.us*) and Sullivan and Rounds (2004).

North Santiam River

For Reach 1, from Detroit Dam to the Little North Santiam River confluence, direct surface-water withdrawals are minimal. The towns of Gates (RM 51.2) and Mill City (RM 47.5) withdraw 0.13 and 0.35 ft^3/s on a mean annual basis, respectively, for municipal water supply. However, downstream from the Little North Santiam River confluence to RM 26 (Reach 2), surface-water withdrawals are more significant. The city of Salem withdraws approximately 67 ft^3/s on a mean annual basis from intakes near Geren Island at RM 31. The city of Stayton and the Santiam Water Control District withdraw approximately 260 ft^3/s on a mean annual basis at RM 29.5. At RM 27.0, NORPAC Foods withdraws 0.40 ft^3/s from June to October. In Reach 3, from RM 26 to the South Santiam River confluence, approximately 40 ft^3/s is withdrawn from May to September by the Sidney Irrigation Cooperative at RM 19.6.

Water-use data for the North Santiam River was used for extending the measured daily mean streamflow time series for the Reach 3 gage, North Santiam River at Green's Bridge near Jefferson (14184100). The period of operation for this station was from water years 1964 to 1967 and 2006 to 2011. To create a longer time series (water years 1951–2011) for this site, daily mean streamflow data from the upstream gage, North Santiam River at Mehama (14183000), were proportionally adjusted to the increased drainage area of the Reach 3 Green's Bridge near Jefferson gage (14184100). These adjusted streamflows

were used to fill in missing periods in the measured (14184100) streamflow time series. Next, all major surface-water withdrawals between the two gages (14183000 and 14184100) were subtracted from the estimated 14184100 streamflow time series. Monthly surface-water withdrawals (2001–2011) for Salem, Stayton Water Control District, NORPAC Foods, and Sidney Irrigation Cooperative were compiled and summed. This amount was offset by effluent from Stayton (3.33 ft^3/s on a mean annual basis) at RM 27.5. Monthly net water withdrawals were converted to daily values and then smoothed using a 30-day running average. Estimated mean annual net water withdrawal between the two gages (14183000 and 14184100) was 335 ft^3/s (water years 2001–2010).

Prior to its subtraction from the estimated streamflow time series for Green's Bridge near Jefferson (14184100), Salem municipal-use withdrawals and Stayton effluent return flows were adjusted for population growth between 1950 and 2011. Using Marion County population for 1950, 1960, 1970, 1980, 1990, 2000, and 2010 from the U.S. Census, a regression was created to estimate the county population for each year from 1950 and 2011. Monthly-mean Salem municipal-use withdrawals and Stayton effluent return flows for the 2001 to 2010 were adjusted to 1950 using a ratio of the population in the earlier year to the population in 2010. However, estimated withdrawals for irrigation use were not adjusted for population growth on the assumption that irrigation use has not increased as rapidly as municipal use has from 1951 to 2011.

South Santiam River

For Reach 4, from Green Peter Dam to Foster Dam, withdrawals from the Middle Santiam River (which flows into the South Santiam River) are minimal or nearly nonexistent. However, in Reach 5, downstream from Foster Dam to RM 23.4, above the Waterloo gage (14187500), mean annual water use reported by the City of Sweet Home was 1.76 ft^3/s for water years 2001–2010. In Reach 6, which extends from the Waterloo gage (14187500) to the North Santiam River confluence, water is diverted from the South Santiam River through the Lebanon-Santiam Canal at RM 20.9, upstream of Lebanon. For water years 1992–2011, mean annual streamflow was 89 ft^3/s as measured at the USGS gage (14187600) on the canal and near the canal diversion point on the river. Since 2007, withdrawals from the river to the canal have been as high as 200 ft^3/s during the summer. The canal water is used for irrigation, small project hydropower generation, and municipal water supply for Lebanon and Albany. Lebanon withdrew 3.01 ft^3/s (average for water years 2001–2010) from the canal (Oregon Water Resources Department, 2012). Previously, the canal diverted water from the South Santiam River at a location slightly downstream from Lebanon at RM 17.0 and was known as the "Albany-Santiam Canal." Mean annual streamflow in the canal during this earlier period was 209 ft^3/s (water years 1926–1957) as measured at the inactive USGS gage (14188000) on the canal.

In addition to the Sweet Home municipal water supply and the Lebanon-Santiam Canal, other substantial diversions in the South Santiam River are for irrigation. From RM 21.1 to the North Santiam River confluence, mean direct surface-water withdrawals for irrigation are 16.9 ft^3/s annually, on the basis of Oregon Water Resources Department water-availability data (Cooper, 2002; Oregon Water Resources Department, 2012).

Main-Stem Santiam River

Surface-water withdrawals in Reach 7, from the confluence of the North and South Santiam Rivers to the Willamette River confluence, include the Jefferson municipal water supply and irrigation for agricultural. Mean annual water use reported by the City of Jefferson was 0.51 ft^3/s for water years 2001–2010. Surface-water withdrawals for irrigation from the Santiam River in Reach 7 are 5.02 ft^3/s on a mean annual basis based on Oregon Water Resources Department water-availability data (Cooper, 2002).

Pre- and Post-Dam Comparisons

Statistical and graphical comparisons were used to assess the effects of dams on streamflows. These included comparisons of annual peak and daily mean streamflow data measured before and after the dams were constructed. Comparisons were also made of post-dam period measured daily mean streamflows with the post-dam period computed unregulated daily mean streamflows provided by the USACE.

Comparisons of pre- and post-dam period measured streamflow data were possible in four of the reaches, which had lengthy continuous streamflow records that began in the 1920s or 1930s. These included North Santiam River at Niagara (14181500), North Santiam River at Mehama (14183000), South Santiam River at Waterloo (14187500), and Santiam River at Jefferson (14189000). In using this method of comparison, it was necessary to determine whether climate was a contributing factor to changes in streamflow by evaluating monthly precipitation data at Salem and Waterloo from the pre- and post-dam periods. On the basis of a Wilcox rank-sum test, there was no significant difference in monthly precipitation between the two periods. The p-values for all the months, with the exception of February in Salem, were greater than 0.5 (table 7).

Table 7. Salem, Oregon, and Waterloo, Oregon, median monthly precipitation totals.

[Source: Western Regional Climate Center (2012). Abbreviation: WY, water year. p-values less than 0.05 resulting from a Wilcox rank-sum test indicate there is a significant difference in the monthly precipitation totals between the pre-dam and post-dam periods. Salem and Waterloo precipitation data from stations 357500 and 359083, respectively.]

	Salem, Oregon (North Santiam River basin)			Waterloo, Oregon (South Santiam River basin)		
	Pre-dam 1935–1952 (inches)	Post-dam 1953–2010 (inches)	p-value	Pre-dam 1935–1966 (inches)	Post-dam 1967–2010 (inches)	p-value
WY total	41.1	39.6	0.56	41.6	45.0	0.34
January	5.34	6.43	0.51	5.29	6.98	0.58
February	5.57	4.28	0.03	4.74	4.41	0.47
March	4.02	3.82	0.92	4.80	4.55	0.78
April	1.88	2.44	0.12	2.62	3.25	0.08
May	1.60	1.90	0.68	1.86	2.20	0.47
June	0.98	1.17	0.47	1.11	1.57	0.06
July	0.36	0.23	0.30	0.03	0.26	0.14
August	0.35	0.38	0.66	0.20	0.57	0.28
September	1.38	1.20	0.83	1.26	1.37	0.19
October	2.87	2.89	0.65	3.30	3.18	0.79
November	5.36	6.05	0.72	6.63	6.47	0.78
December	6.25	6.95	1.00	5.59	7.13	0.59

Statistical metrics representing different environmental flow components, such as low flows (7-day annual minimum, 95-percent exceedance), high flows (1-day maximum annual, 5-percent exceedence), floods (annual peak), and median monthly flows, were computed to compare pre- and post-dam conditions.

Graphical comparisons of pre- and post-streamflow regulation include mean daily streamflow plots. Mean daily streamflow for any one day, October 10, for example, is the arithmetic mean of the discharge on all October 10s of the record, or a specified period of a record. This is different from daily mean streamflow, which is defined as the mean streamflow for that one day. Because a mean daily streamflow plot dampens

the magnitude of floods, comparisons of measured daily mean streamflows and USACE computed unregulated daily streamflows for a single water year (1975) also were included. Water year 1975 data were used in the daily mean streamflow comparison plots because it approximates an average year in the historic streamflow record (water years 1939–2011) for the Santiam River at Jefferson (14189000).

Streamflow Assessment

Results from an assessment of the effects of dams and surface-water withdrawals on the full streamflow regime for the seven study reaches in the Santiam River basin are described below.

North Santiam River

The hydrologic effect of the Detroit and Big Cliff Dams, completed in 1953, is evident in the streamflow record at the USGS gage on the North Santiam River at Mehama (14183000) (fig. 6). Prior to dam regulation, daily mean streamflow exceeded the USACE defined bankfull (17,000 ft³/s) and flood (30,500 ft³/s) threshold discharges on average 3.39 and 0.68 times per year, respectively, from 1922 to 1952. However, from 1953 to 2011, bankfull and flood threshold discharges were exceeded on average only 0.97 and 0.03 times per year, respectively. The two times the

flood threshold was exceeded in the post-dam period were December 22, 1964, at 36,200 ft³/s and February 7, 1996, at 46,700 ft³/s, respectively. The USACE estimated that these two events would have been 91,600 and 96,400 ft³/s, respectively, had the dams not been constructed (fig. 6) (Alan Donner, U.S. Army Corps of Engineers, written commun., 2011).

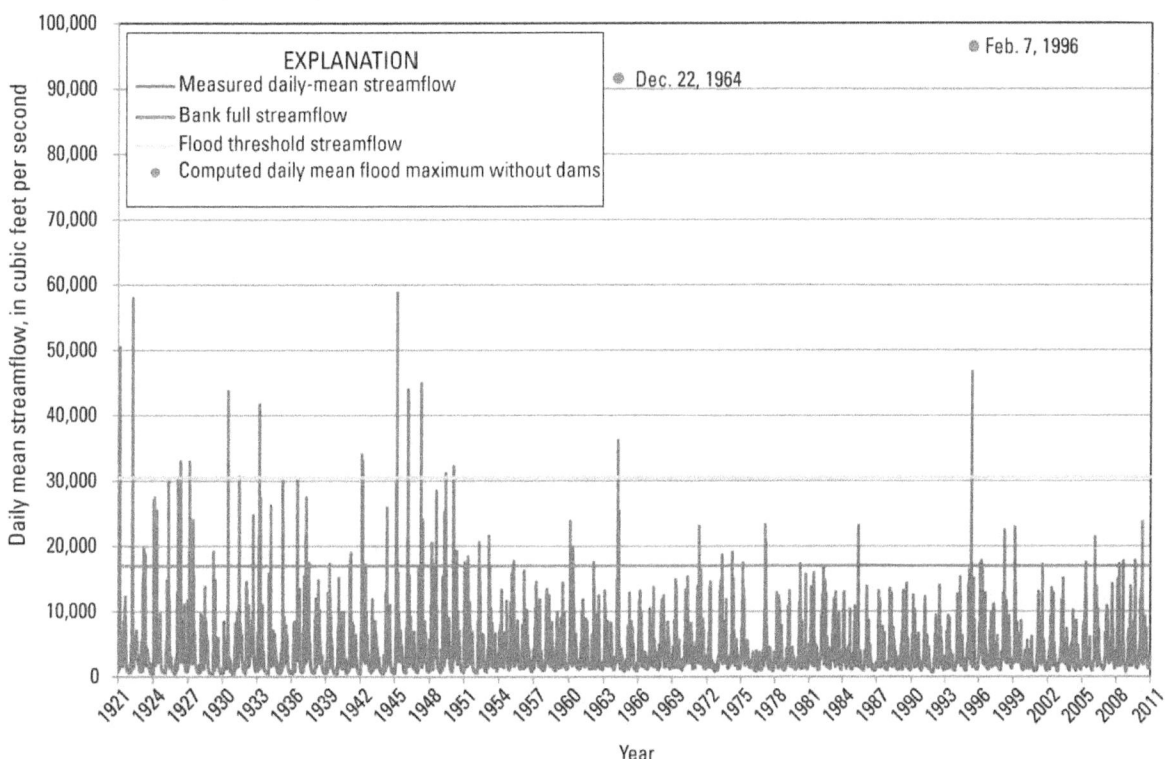

Figure 6. Graph showing daily mean streamflow in Reach 2 at North Santiam River at Mehama, Oregon (14183000), water years 1922–2011.

A comparison of measured and computed unregulated mean daily streamflows (water years 1953–2009) at North Santiam River gages in Reaches 1–3 at Niagara (14181500), Mehama (14183000), and Green's Bridge (14184100) showed that February–April streamflows decreased and August–November streamflows increased under regulated streamflow conditions

(figs. 7–9), respectively. These streamflow alterations are typical of locations downstream from reservoirs used for hydropower production and flood control. Flows are decreased in the spring when the reservoirs are filling up. The increased fall flows are the result of reservoir drawdown each year prior to the annual flood season.

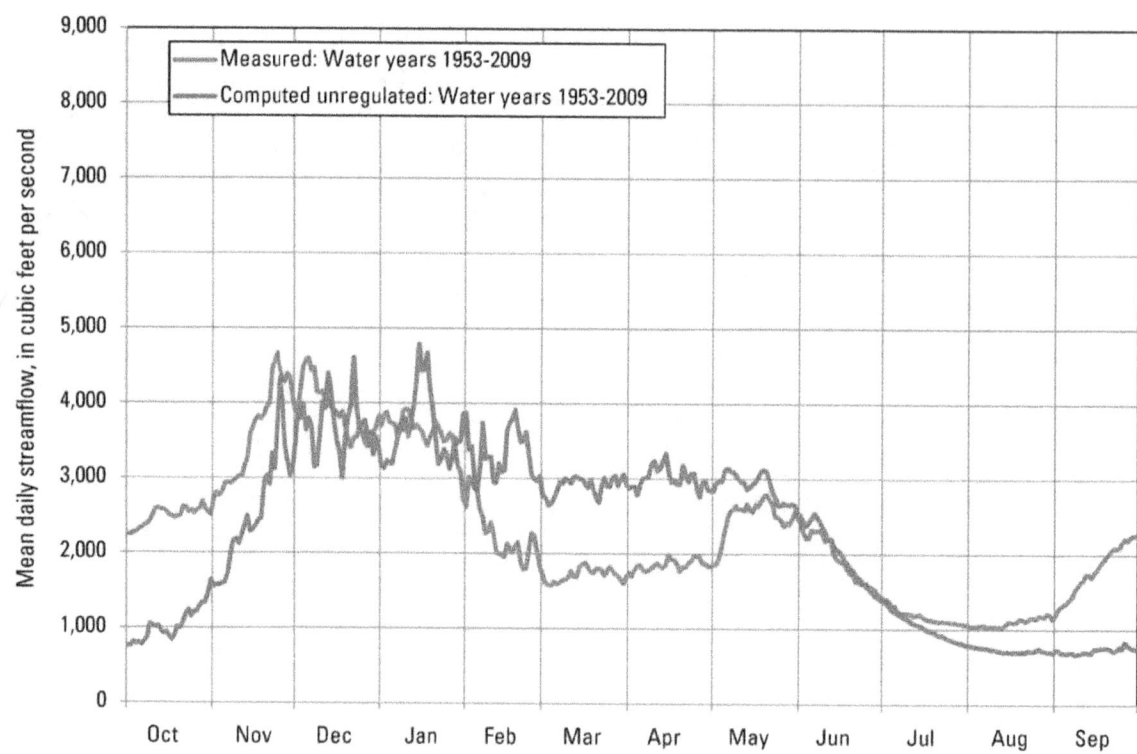

Figure 7. Graph showing mean daily streamflow in Reach 1 at North Santiam River at Niagara, Oregon (14181500), water years 1953–2009.

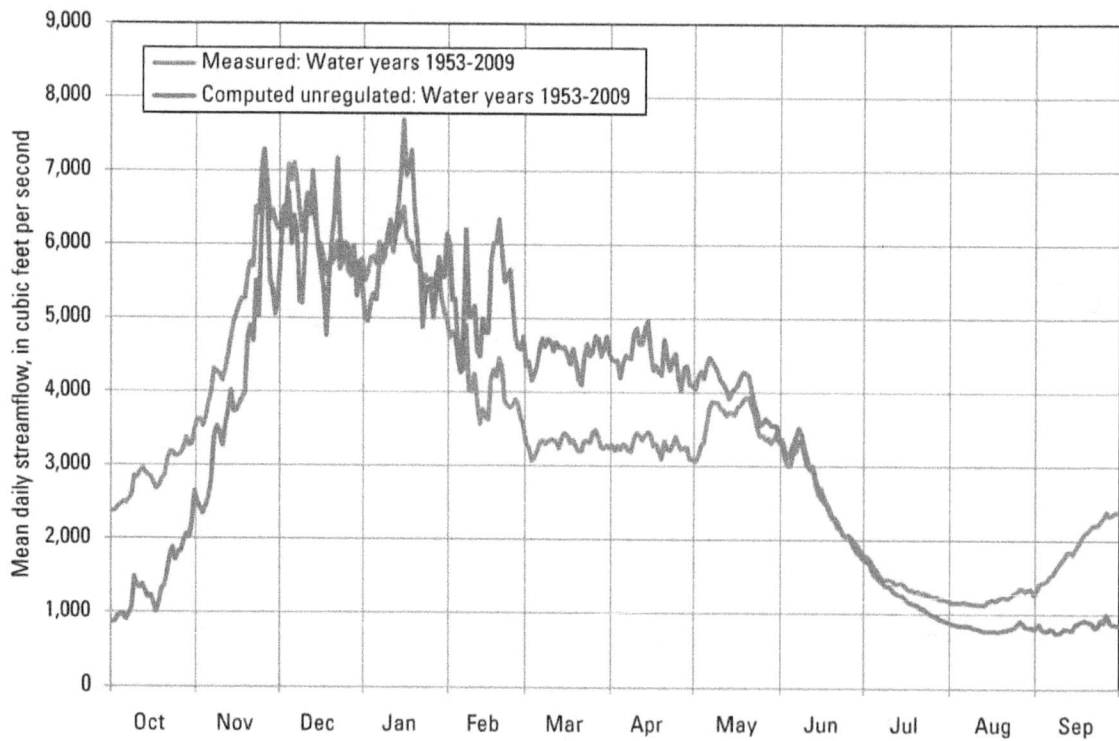

Figure 8. Graph showing mean daily streamflow in Reach 2 at North Santiam River at Mehama, Oregon (14183000), water years 1953–2009.

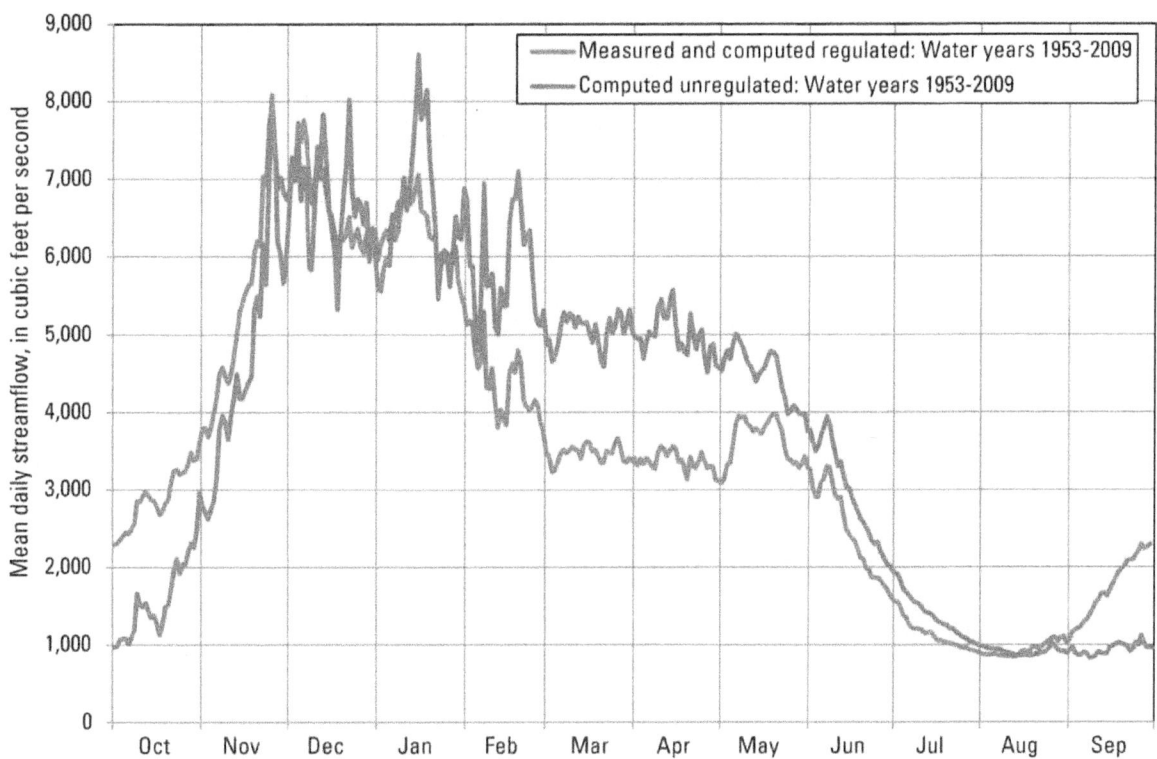

Figure 9. Graph showing mean daily streamflow in Reach 3 at North Santiam River at Green's Bridge near Jefferson, Oregon (14184100), water years 1953–2009.

Changes in seasonal streamflow patterns caused by the dams is also evident in a comparison of measured regulated and computed unregulated daily mean streamflows at these three gages during a single average hydrologic year (1975). Although the timing of high-flow events remained constant, the magnitude of these events decreased. The dam operation and its effect on streamflow can be seen at Niagara (14181500) (fig. 10), particularly in March and April and again in August and September. The effect of dam operation on streamflow becomes dampened at the two downstream gages (figs. 11–12).

Using annual peak-flow data, flood frequencies based on the Bulletin 17B Log Pearson III method were computed for the pre-dam and post-dam periods for Niagara (14181500) and Mehama (14183000). The period of record for peak-flow measurements is longer, extending to 1909 for Niagara (14181500) and to 1906 for Mehama (14183000), than the period of record for collection of continuous discharge at these stations. For both gages, the 1.5-, 10-, 50-, 100-, and 500-year peak flows decreased in the post-dam period (1953–2010) (table 8). The range of decrease in peak flows was greater for the Niagara (14181500) gage (-43 – -81 percent) than the Mehama (14183000) gage (-38 – -44 percent).

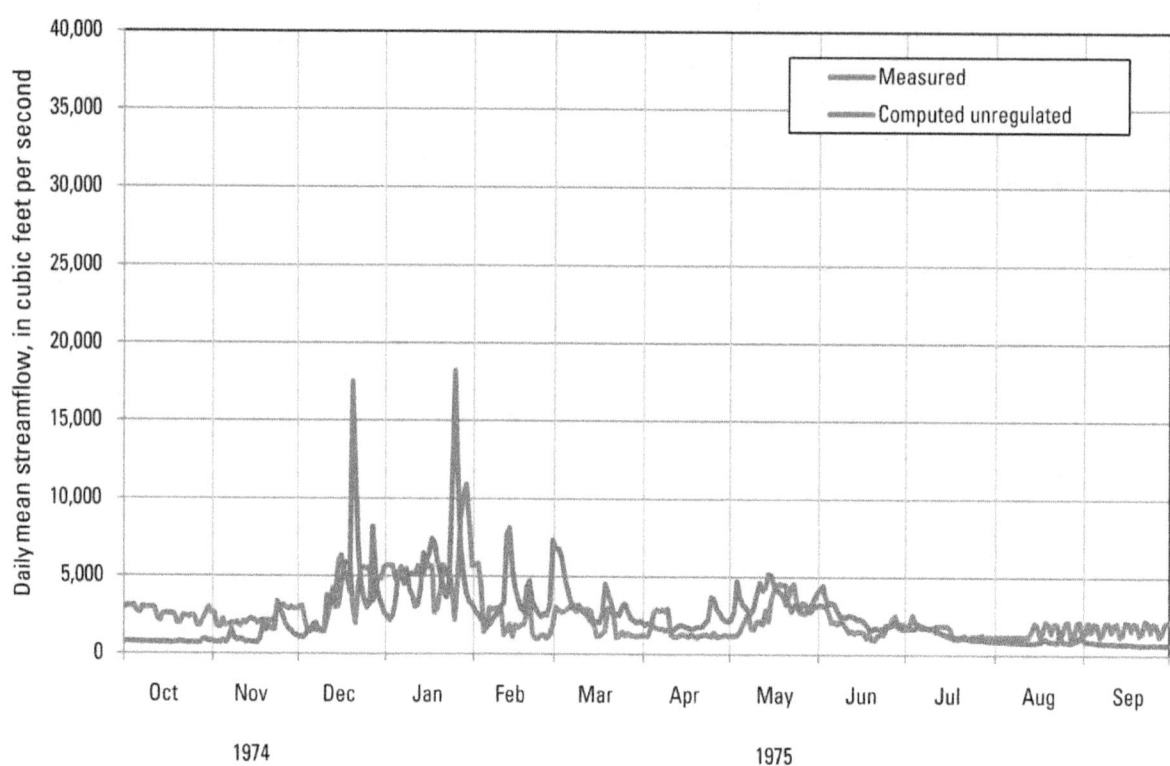

Figure 10. Graph showing daily mean streamflow in Reach 1 at North Santiam River at Niagara, Oregon (14181500), water year 1975.

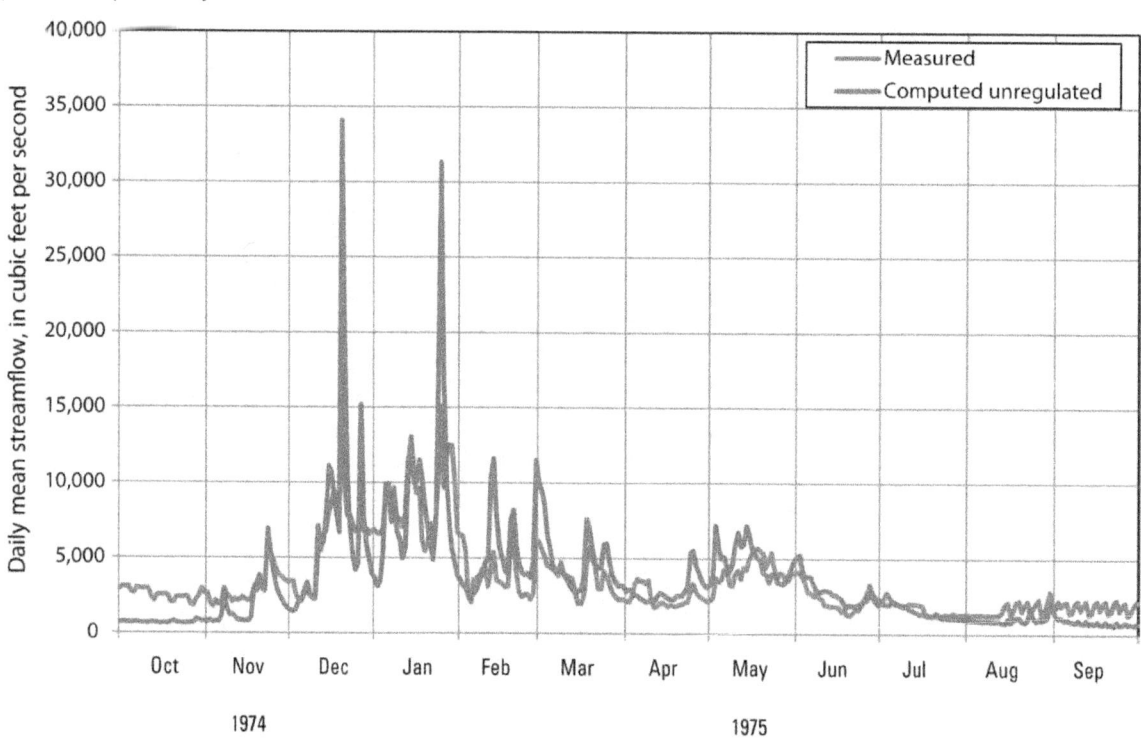

Figure 11. Graph showing daily mean streamflow in Reach 2 at North Santiam River at Mehama, Oregon (14183000), water year 1975.

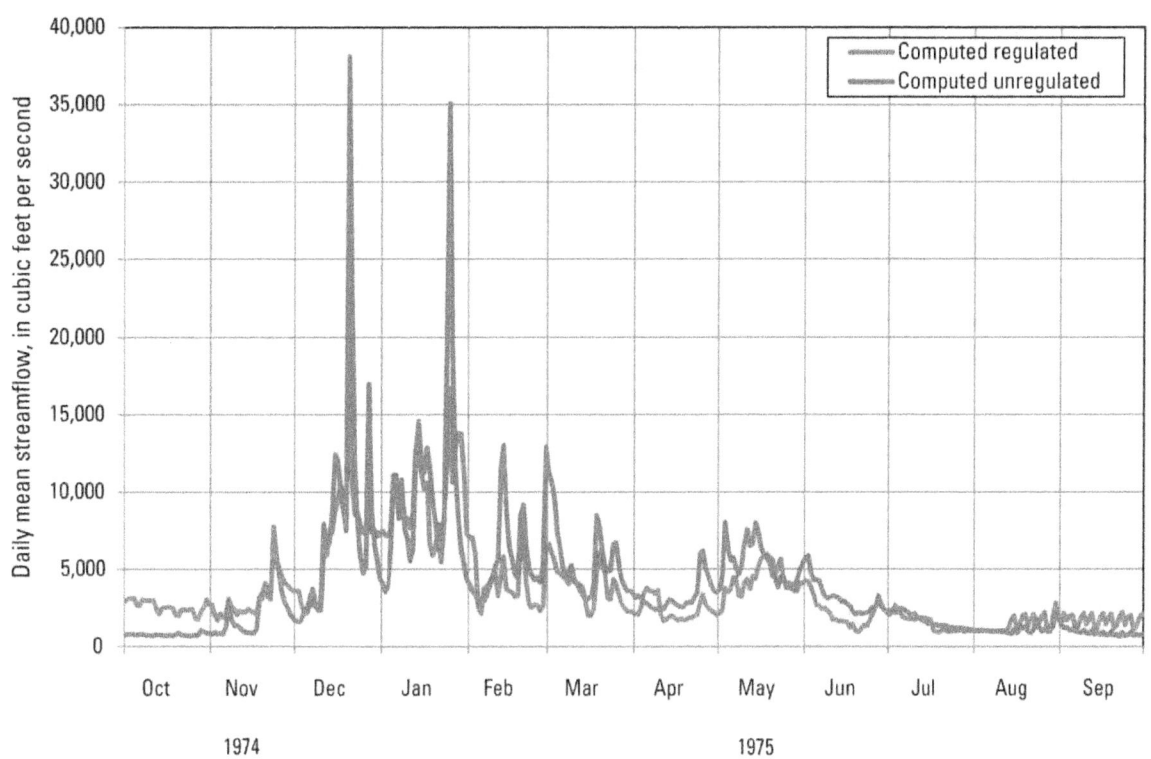

Figure 12. Graph showing daily mean streamflow in Reach 3 at North Santiam River at Green's Bridge near Jefferson, Oregon (14184100), water year 1975.

Table 8. Pre- and post-dam flood statistics for selected Santiam River basin, Oregon, streamflow gaging stations, computed from annual peak streamflow data based on the Bulletin 17B Log Pearson III method.

[**Abbreviations**: POR, period of record in water years; ft^3/s, cubic feet per second.]

| Station number | Streamflow gaging-station name and study reach number | Recurrence interval (years) | Pre-dam period | | Post-dam period | | Percent change |
			POR	Streamflow (ft^3/s)	POR	Streamflow (ft^3/s)	
14181500	North Santiam River at Niagara, Oregon, Reach 1	1.5	1909–1952	16,700	1953–2010	9,540	-43
		10		44,700		15,200	-66
		50		69,600		18,000	-74
		100		81,300		19,000	-77
		500		111,000		21,100	-81
14183000	North Santiam River at Mehama, Oregon, Reach 2	1.5	1906–1952	28,500	1953–2010	17,800	-38
		10		58,300		32,700	-44
		50		79,800		45,500	-43
		100		89,000		51,500	-42
		500		111,000		67,200	-39
14187500	South Santiam River at Waterloo, Oregon, Reach 6	1.5	1906–1966	31,500	1967–2010	14,200	-55
		10		65,600		20,900	-68
		50		91,300		24,800	-73
		100		103,000		26,300	-74
		500		130,000		29,700	-77
14189000	Santiam River at Jefferson, Oregon, Reach 7	1.5	1908–1952	62,400	1953–2010	44,200	-29
		10		152,000		102,000	-33
		50		231,000		157,000	-32
		100		268,000		184,000	-31
		500		364,000		259,000	-29

Under regulated streamflow conditions, the median of annual 1-day maximum streamflows at the three North Santiam River gages at Niagara (14181500), Mehama (14183000), and Green's Bridge (14184100) decreased by 42 to 50 percent for 1953–2009 compared to computed unregulated streamflow conditions (table 9). In contrast, the median of annual 7-day minimum streamflows increased by 25 to 93 percent at these three stations (table 10). The median monthly streamflows at all three gages decreased in the late winter and spring (February–June) and all increased in the late summer to winter (September–January) (table 11). For the Reach 1 and 2 gages,

Niagara (14181500) and Mehama (14183000), respectively, median monthly streamflows increased in July and August as a result of dam regulation. However, for Reach 3, median monthly streamflows decreased in July and August, because the regulated streamflow time series, based on measured data, includes surface-water withdrawals for municipal water use and irrigation in Reach 3. The unregulated time series, computed by the USACE, does not take into account these withdrawals because it was created for the purpose of quantifying the effects of the dams on streamflow.

Table 9. One-day maximum annual streamflow statistics from regulated and unregulated daily mean streamflows for the Santiam River, Oregon.

[Regulated and unregulated streamflows based on observed and computed data as described in the text. Medians computed from the 1-day maximum annual flows for the period of record.]

Reach number	Station number	Streamflow gaging station name	Period of record (water years)	Unregulated streamflow median (ft³/s)	Regulated streamflow median (ft³/s)	Percent change
1	14181500	North Santiam River at Niagara, Oregon	1953–2009	17,900	10,300	-42
2	14183000	North Santiam River at Mehama, Oregon	1953–2009	28,700	14,500	-49
3	14184100	North Santiam River at Greens Bridge near Jefferson, Oregon	1953–2009	32,200	16,000	-50
4	14186500	Middle Santiam River at mouth near Foster, Oregon	1967–2009	16,400	9,950	-39
5	14186700	South Santiam River at Foster, Oregon	1967–2009	24,900	11,900	-52
6	14187500	South Santiam River at Waterloo, Oregon	1967–2009	27,700	13,600	-51
7	14189000	Santiam River at Jefferson, Oregon	1953–2009	71,800	43,900	-39

Table 10. Seven-day minimum annual streamflow statistics from regulated and unregulated daily mean streamflows for the Santiam River, Oregon.

[Regulated and unregulated streamflows based on observed and computed data as described in the text. Medians were computed from the 7-day minimum annual flows for the period of records.]

Reach number	Station number	Streamflow gaging station name	Period of record (water years)	Unregulated streamflow median (ft³/s)	Regulated streamflow median (ft³/s)	Percent change
1	14181500	North Santiam River at Niagara, Oregon	1953–2009	579	928	60
2	14183000	North Santiam River at Mehama, Oregon	1953–2009	554	1,070	93
3	14184100	North Santiam River at Greens Bridge near Jefferson, Oregon	1953–2009	620	773	25
4	14186500	Middle Santiam River at mouth near Foster, Oregon	1967–2009	85.6	52.6	-39
5	14186700	South Santiam River at Foster, Oregon	1967–2009	155	636	310
6	14187500	South Santiam River at Waterloo, Oregon	1967–2009	145	631	335
7	14189000	Santiam River at Jefferson, Oregon	1953–2009	359	1,210	237

Table 11. Median monthly streamflow statistics from regulated and unregulated daily mean streamflows for the Santiam River, Oregon.

[POR, Period of record; WY, water year from October 1 to September 30. ft³/s, cubic feet per second. Regulated and unregulated streamflows based on observed and computed data as described in the text. Medians computed from monthly flows for the period of records.]

Reach number	Station number	POR in WY	Streamflow condition	January (ft³/s)	February (ft³/s)	March (ft³/s)	April (ft³/s)	May (ft³/s)	June (ft³/s)	July (ft³/s)	August (ft³/s)	September (ft³/s)	October (ft³/s)	November (ft³/s)	December (ft³/s)
1	14181500	1953–2009	Unregulated	2,610	2,400	2,420	2,710	2,660	1,700	937	687	665	760	1,720	2,470
			Regulated	2,900	1,090	1,050	1,420	2,220	1,530	1,090	1,020	1,780	2,360	3,060	3,020
			Percent change	11	-55	-57	-48	-17	-10	16	48	168	211	78	22
2	14183000	1953–2009	Unregulated	4,180	3,680	3,740	3,980	3,610	2,160	1,090	755	721	891	2,670	3,930
			Regulated	5,050	2,690	2,530	2,780	3,270	2,070	1,270	1,120	1,880	2,490	4,140	5,350
			Percent change	21	-27	-32	-30	-9	-4	17	48	161	179	55	36
3	14184100	1953–2009	Unregulated	4,680	4,120	4,190	4,450	4,040	2,420	1,220	845	807	998	2,990	4,400
			Regulated	5,460	2,820	2,630	2,850	3,250	1,880	983	830	1,710	2,480	4,400	5,780
			Percent change	17	-32	-37	-36	-20	-22	-19	-2	112	148	47	31
4	14186500	1967–2009	Unregulated	2,340	1,880	1,960	1,880	1,410	641	228	126	147	273	1,560	2,350
			Regulated	2,660	526	568	993	1,290	673	599	631	1,060	1,340	2,310	3,570
			Percent change	14	-72	-71	-47	-9	5	163	401	621	391	48	52
5	14186700	1967–2009	Unregulated	3,660	2,970	3,020	3,010	2,250	1,030	377	210	228	426	2,340	3,680
			Regulated	4,390	1,680	1,700	2,220	1,770	1,040	743	708	1,110	1,560	3,300	5,350
			Percent change	20	-43	-44	-26	-21	1	97	237	387	266	41	45
6	14187500	1967–2009	Unregulated	4,220	3,570	3,710	3,540	2,500	1,120	388	206	251	489	2,650	4,270
			Regulated	5,180	2,390	2,360	2,760	2,050	1,120	771	691	1,150	1,660	3,570	6,000
			Percent change	23	-33	-36	-22	-18	0	99	235	358	239	35	41
7	14189000	1953–2009	Unregulated	10,800	9,370	9,270	9,020	6,940	3,470	1,160	551	639	1,280	6,060	10,300
			Regulated	12,700	7,960	7,330	7,270	6,280	3,520	1,690	1,370	2,480	3,920	8,550	13,000
			Percent change	18	-15	-21	-19	-10	1	46	149	288	206	41	26

For the Reach 1 gage, North Santiam River at Niagara (14181500), the 5-percent streamflow exceedance under regulation decreased by about 6 percent (table 12). Changes in the 5-percent streamflow exceedance as a consequence of regulation at the Reach 2 and 3 gages, Mehama (14183000) and Green's Bridge (14184100), were less than 2 percent (table 12 and figs. 13–15). For low-flow periods, the 95-percent streamflow exceedance increased for all three of the North Santiam River gages by 13 to 75 percent. This is typical for low flows with reservoir regulation. It is also noteworthy that the increase in low flows is less noticeable at the Reach 3 gage because of major water withdrawals between the Reach 2 and 3 gages (fig. 15).

Table 12. Streamflow exceedance statistics from regulated and unregulated daily mean streamflows for the Santiam River, Oregon.

[POR, Period of record; WY, water year from Oct. 1 to Sept. 30. cfs, cubic feet per second. Regulated and unregulated streamflows based on observed and computed data as described in the text.]

Reach number	Station number	POR in WY	Streamflow condition	Percent of daily mean streamflow, in cubic feet per second, equaled or exceeded						
				5	10	25	50	75	90	95
1	14181500	1953–2009	Unregulated	5,910	4,380	2,810	1,680	864	635	583
			Regulated	5,560	4,640	2,880	1,680	1,050	958	900
			Percent change	-5.9	5.8	2.4	0.2	21	51	54
2	14183000	1953–2009	Unregulated	9,660	6,870	4,270	2,420	1,040	685	593
			Regulated	9,680	6,970	4,130	2,450	1,590	1,150	1,040
			Percent change	0.2	1.4	-3.3	1.3	53	68	75
3	14184100	1953–2009	Unregulated	10,800	7,680	4,780	2,710	1,170	767	663
			Regulated	10,600	7,520	4,420	2,430	1,440	882	752
			Percent change	-1.8	-2.1	-7.5	-10	23	15	13
4	14186500	1967–2009	Unregulated	5,770	3,890	2,190	1,050	263	126	97
			Regulated	4,940	4,310	2,130	1,040	557	294	53
			Percent change	-14	11	-2.7	-1.0	112	133	-46
5	14186700	1967–2009	Unregulated	8,730	5,950	3,410	1,640	421	208	167
			Regulated	8,930	6,130	3,230	1,530	830	686	612
			Percent change	2.3	3.0	-5.3	-6.7	97	230	266
6	14187500	1967–2009	Unregulated	9,880	6,880	4,000	1,950	470	222	164
			Regulated	10,300	7,050	3,810	1,840	957	709	629
			Percent change	4.2	2.5	-4.7	-5.6	104	220	283
7	14189000	1953–2009	Unregulated	24,600	17,000	10,100	5,120	1,280	551	386
			Regulated	25,100	17,500	9,750	5,120	2,570	1,480	1,200
			Percent change	2.0	3.1	-3.2	0.1	100	169	211

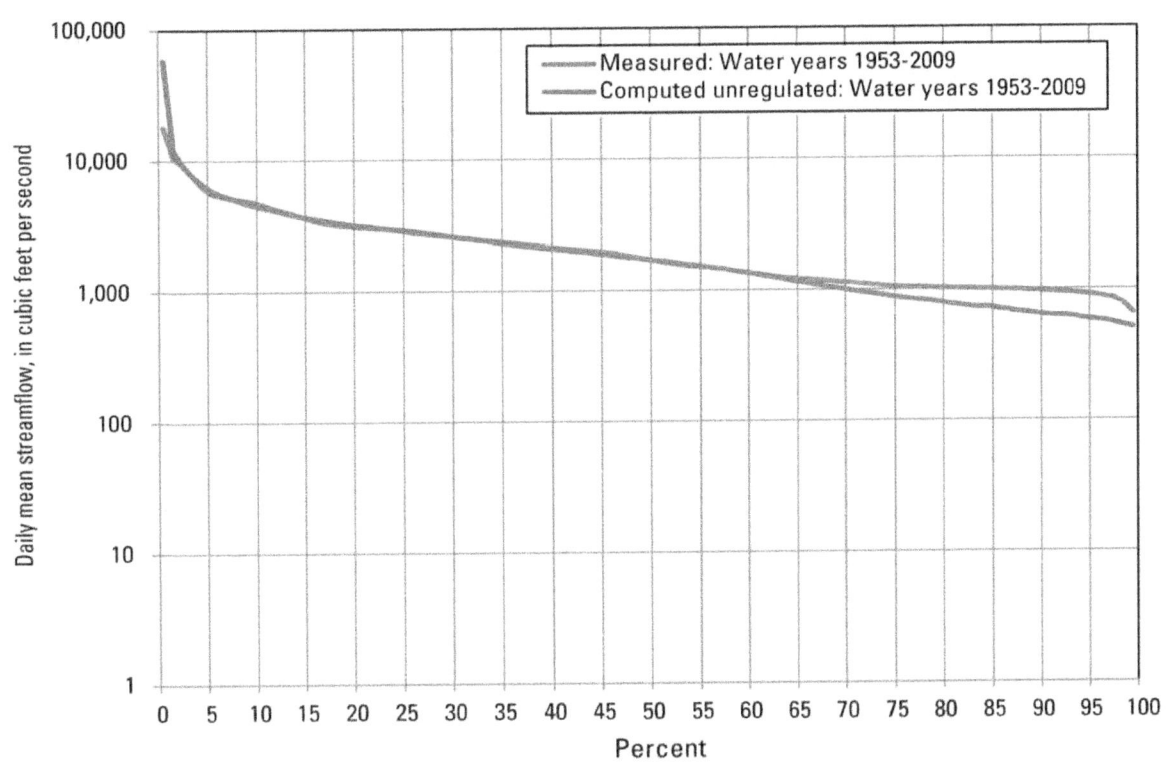

Figure 13. Graph showing percent of daily mean streamflows equaled or exceeded in Reach 1 at North Santiam River at Niagara, Oregon (14181500), water years 1953–2009.

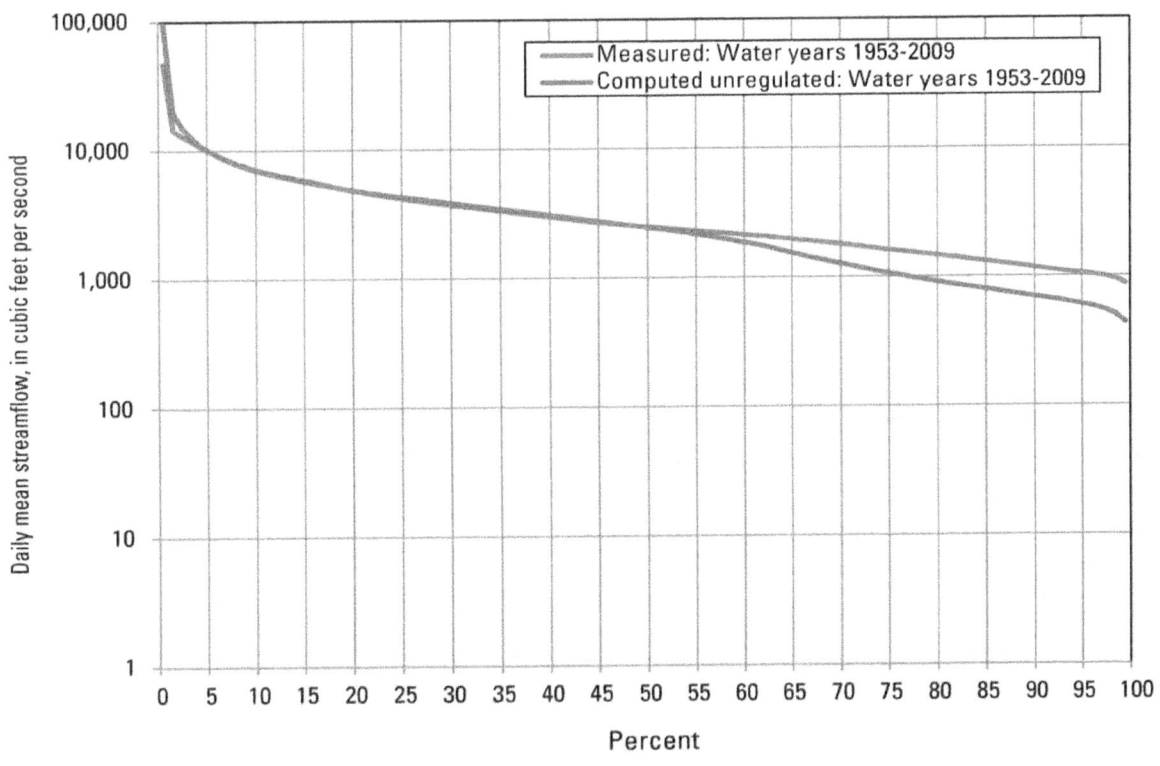

Figure 14. Graph showing percent of daily mean streamflows equaled or exceeded in Reach 2 at North Santiam River at Mehama, Oregon (14183000), water years 1953–2009.

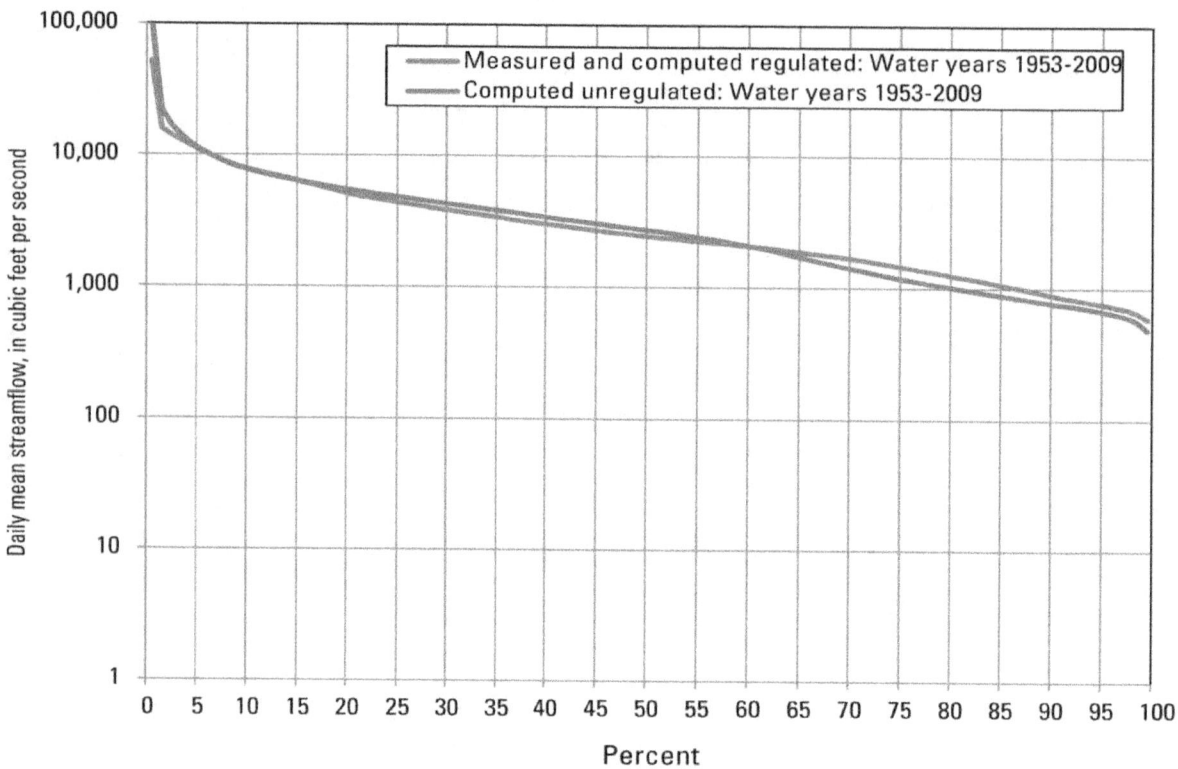

Figure 15. Graph showing percent of daily mean streamflows equaled or exceeded in Reach 3 at North Santiam River at Green's Bridge near Jefferson, Oregon (14184100), water years 1953–2009.

South Santiam River

The longest streamflow time series in the South Santiam River basin was recorded at South Santiam River at Waterloo (14187500), which has been in continuous operation since 1923 (fig. 16). The highest daily mean streamflow in the record was on December 22, 1964, at 77,000 ft^3/s prior to the construction of the Green Peter and Foster Dams in 1967. Prior to dam regulation, daily mean streamflow exceeded the USACE defined bankfull and flood threshold discharges on average 4.12 and 1.72 times per year, respectively, for the period from the start of water year 1924 to the end of water year 1966. For water years 1967–2011, bankfull and flood threshold

discharges were exceeded on average only 0.18 and 0.02 times per year, respectively. The one time the flood threshold was exceeded in the post-dam period was February 7, 1996, at 24,200 ft^3/s. If the dams had not been constructed, the USACE estimated that this event would have been 83,800 ft^3/s at Waterloo (14187500).

Using annual peak flows, which have been measured at the Waterloo (14187500) gage since 1906, flood frequencies were separately computed for the pre-dam (1906–1966) and post-dam (1967–2010) periods. As a result of dam regulation, the 1.5-, 10-, 50-, 100-, and 500-year peak flows decreased by 55 to 77 percent (table 8).

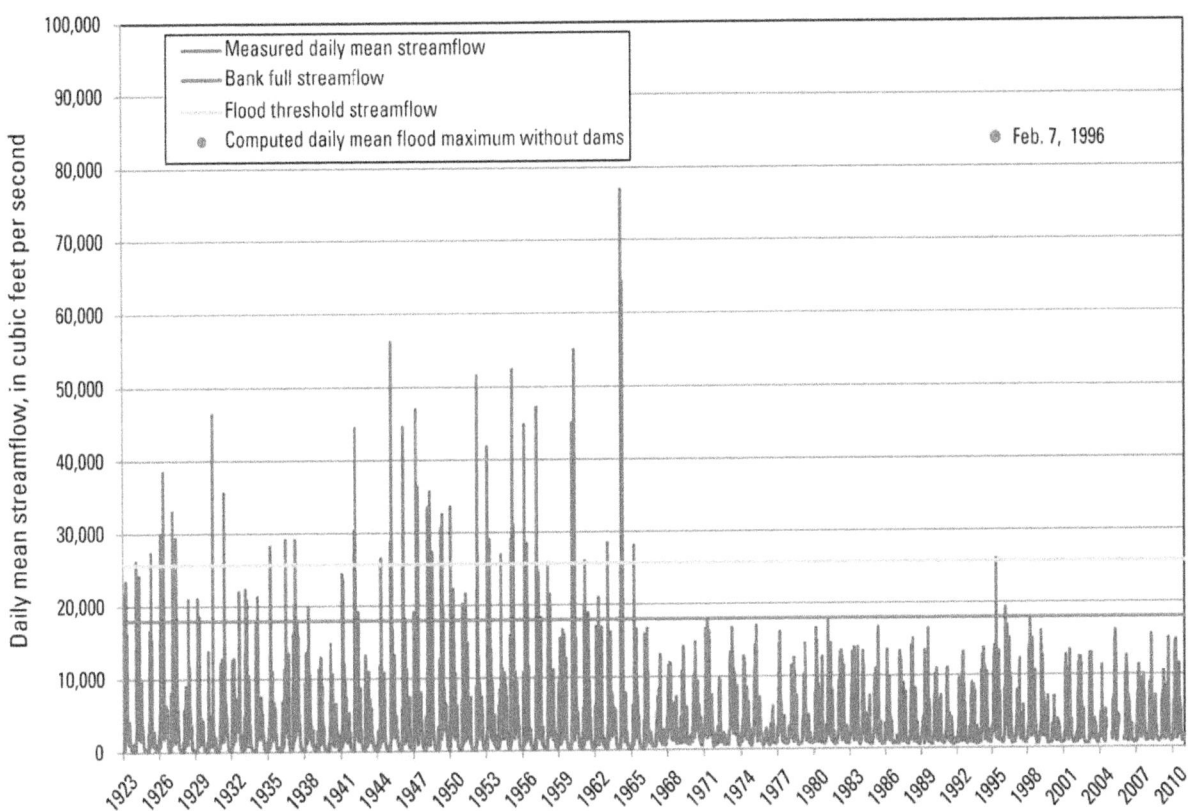

Figure 16. Graph showing daily mean streamflow in Reach 6 at South Santiam River at Waterloo, Oregon (14187500), water years 1924–2011.

Following a similar pattern as the North Santiam gages, a comparison of measured and computed unregulated mean daily streamflows (water years 1967–2009) at the three South Santiam River basin gages (Reaches 4–6) showed that February–May streamflows decreased and July–November streamflows increased under regulated streamflow conditions (figs. 17–19). The Middle Santiam River at mouth near Foster (14186500)

gage (Reach 4) shows the effects of regulation from Green Peter Dam. The Reach 5 gage is on the South Santiam River at Foster (14186700) just below Foster Dam. Farther downstream, in Reach 6, the streamflow record for Waterloo (14187500) at RM 23.3 shows the effects of Foster Dam streamflow regulation combined with unregulated inflow from Wiley, Ames, and McDowell Creeks.

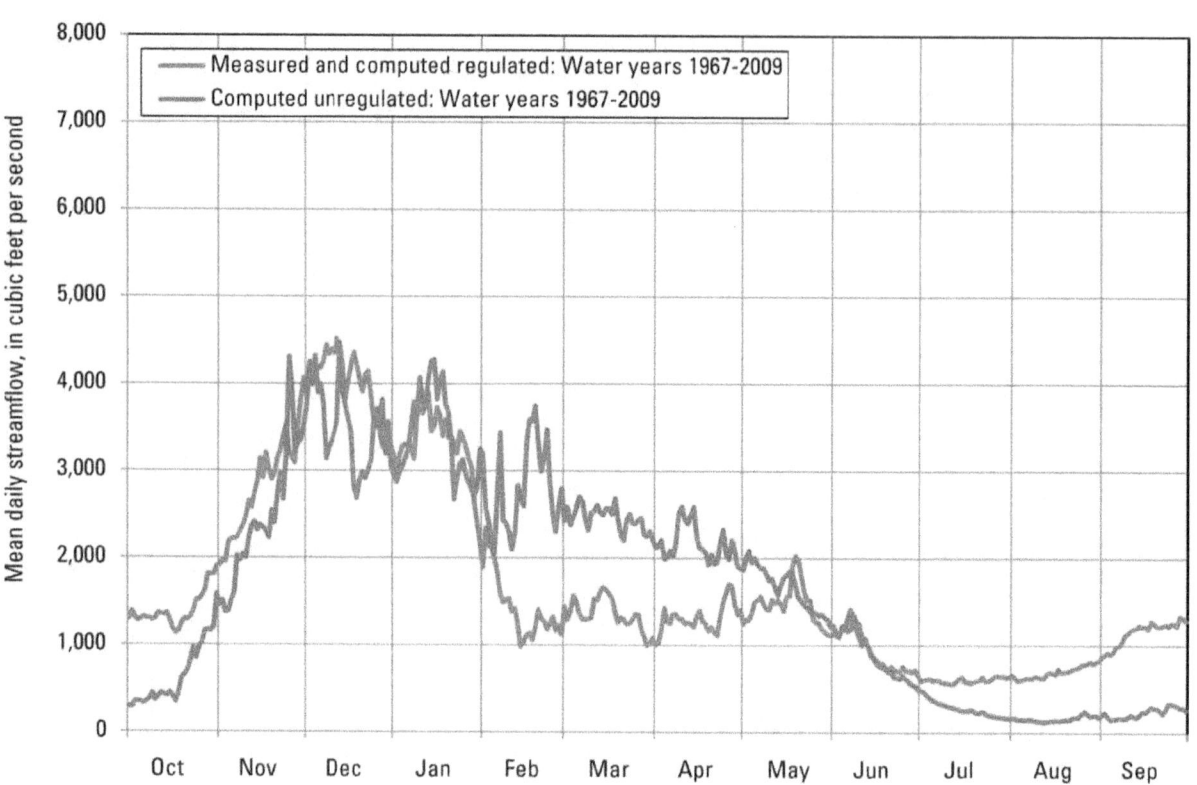

Figure 17. Graph showing mean daily streamflow in Reach 4 at Middle Santiam River at mouth near Foster, Oregon (14186500), water years 1967–2009.

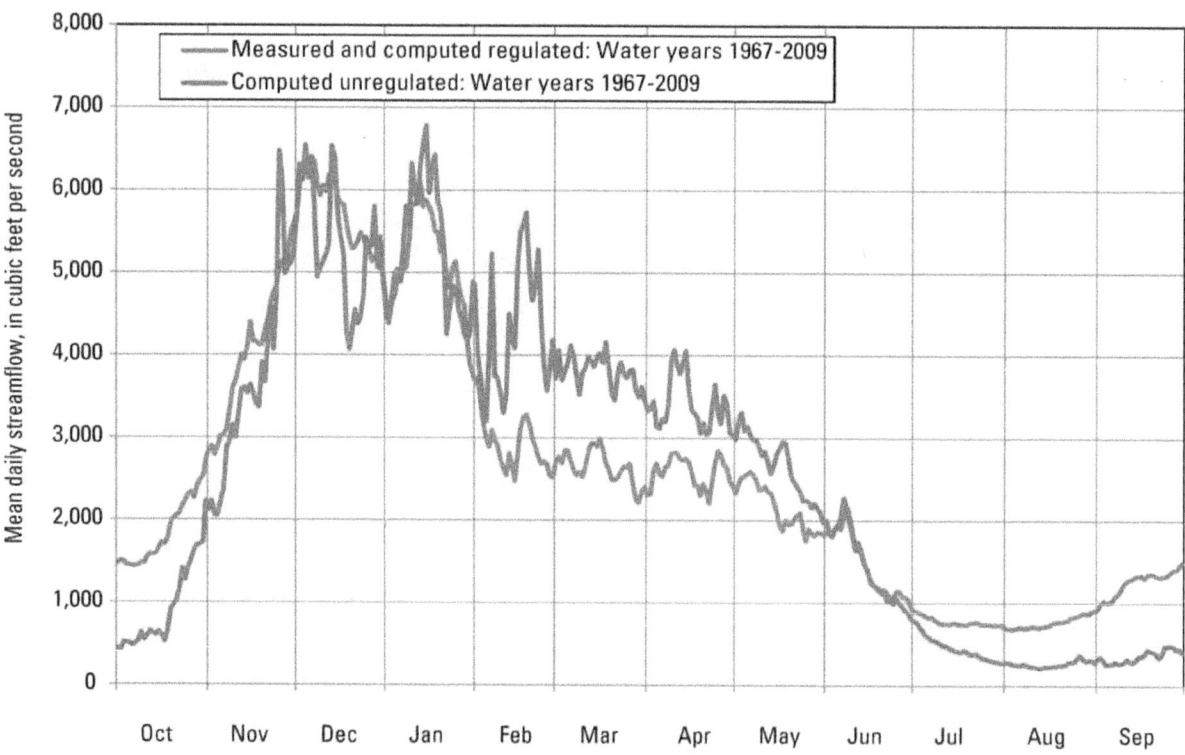

Figure 18. Graph showing mean daily streamflow in Reach 5 at South Santiam River at Foster, Oregon (14186700), water years 1967–2009.

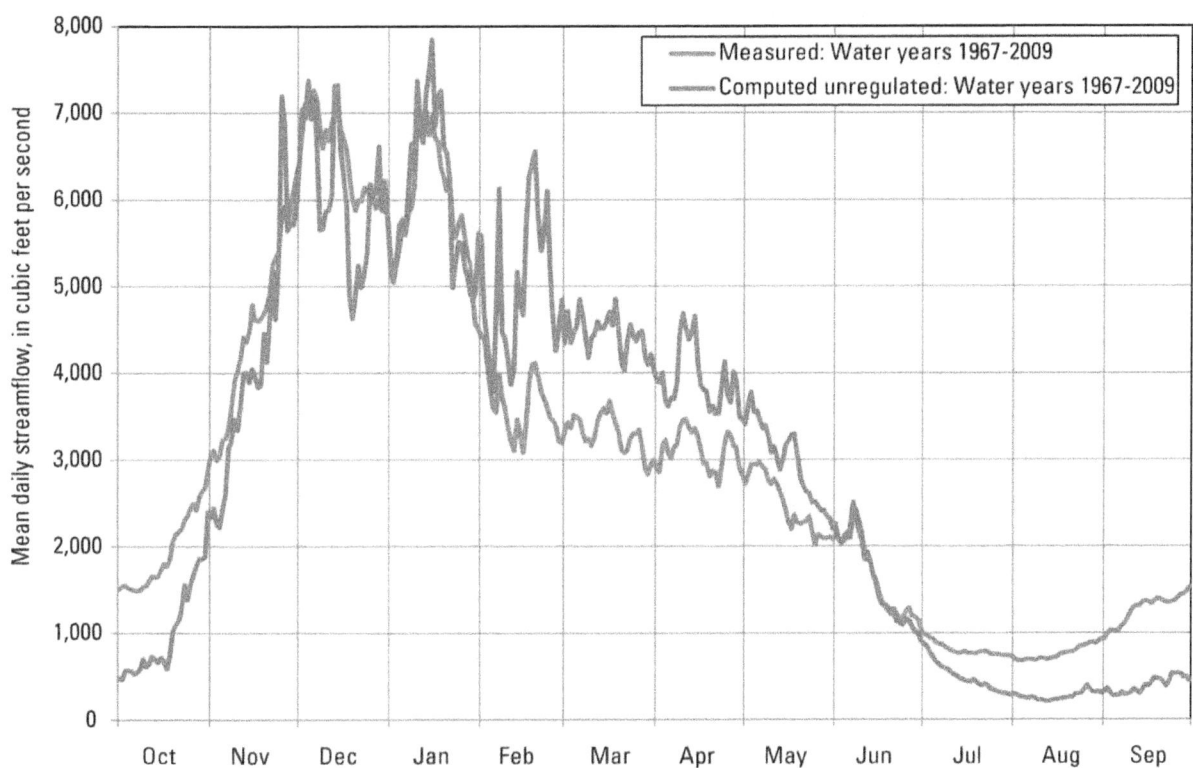

Figure 19. Graph showing mean daily streamflow in Reach 6 at South Santiam River at Waterloo, Oregon (14187500), water years 1967–2009.

A comparison of measured regulated and computed unregulated daily mean streamflows at these three gages (Reaches 4–6) during a single average hydrologic year (1975) showed the effects of dam regulation in the annual hydrograph (figs. 20–22). Green Peter Dam operation and its effect on streamflow at the Reach 4 gage (14186500) (fig. 20) is evident in comparison to the measured streamflow at the Reach 5 gage (14186700) (fig. 21), which is below Foster Dam. Because one of the objectives of Foster Dam is re-regulating Green Peter Dam discharge, measured streamflow below Foster Dam appears more natural and less regulated than streamflow from Green Peter Dam.

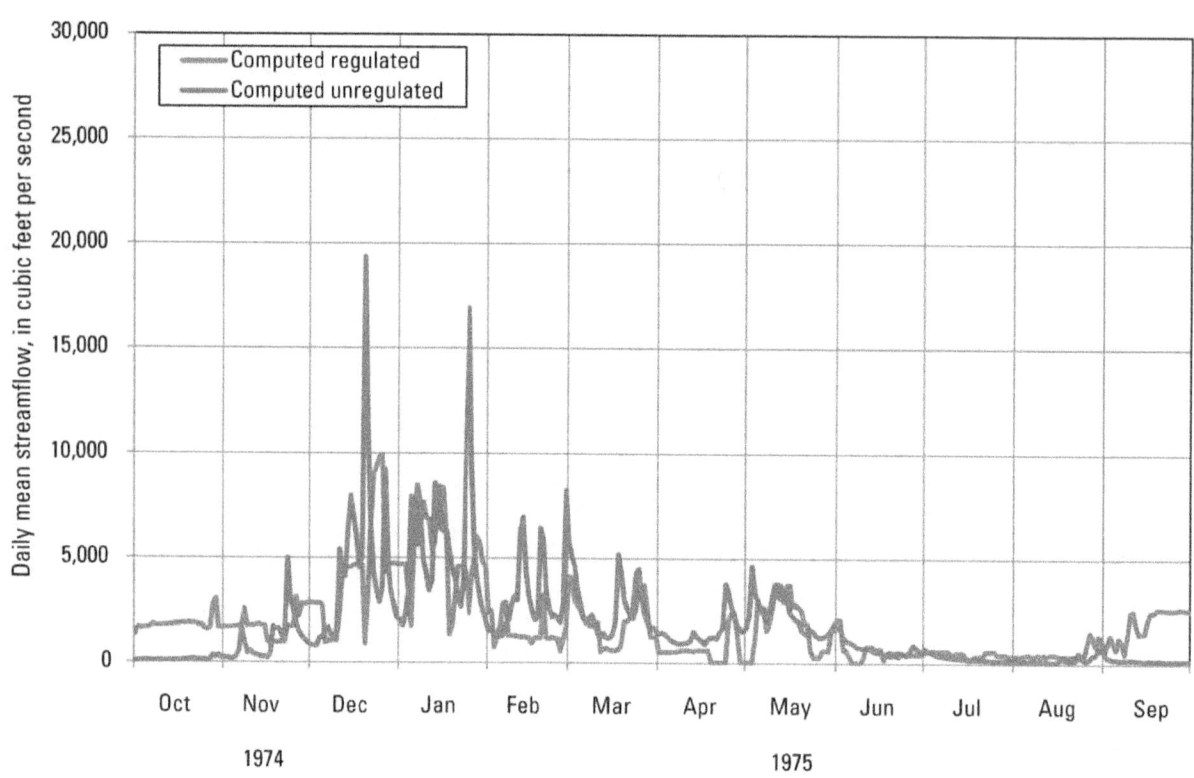

Figure 20. Graph showing daily mean streamflow in Reach 4 at Middle Santiam River at mouth near Foster, Oregon (14186500), water year 1975.

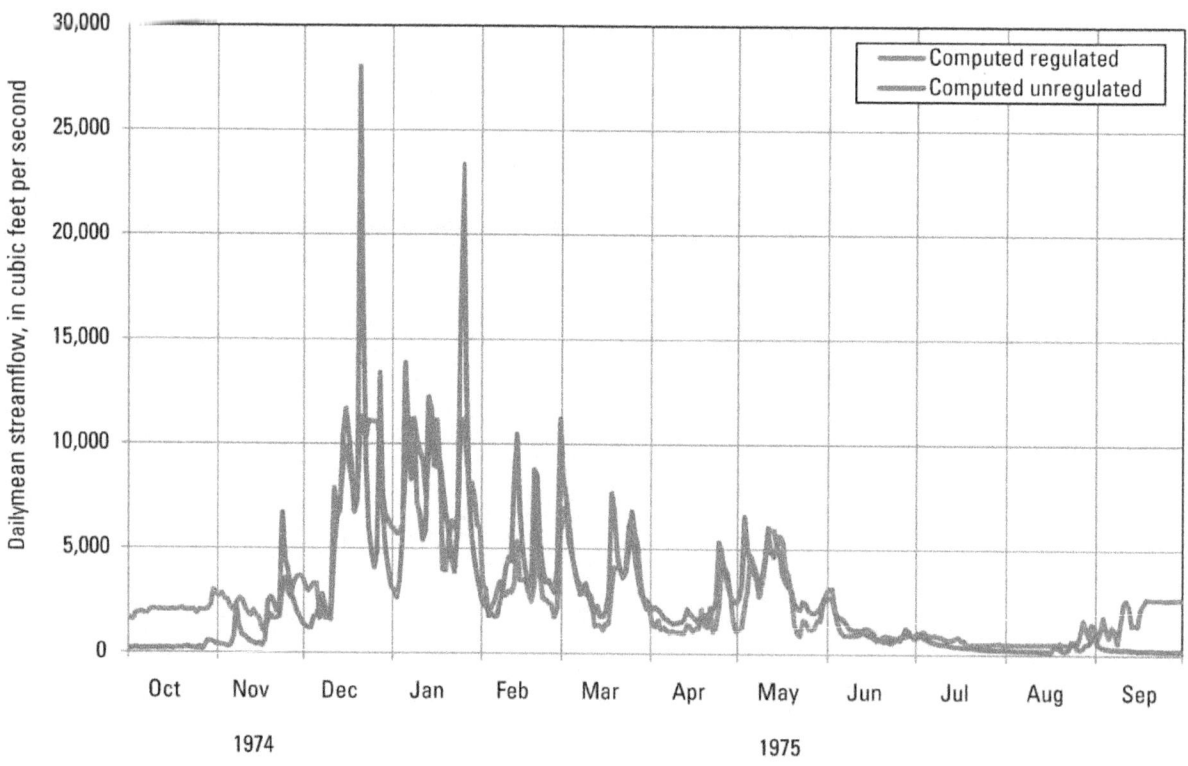

Figure 21. Graph showing daily mean streamflow in Reach 5 at South Santiam River at Foster, Oregon (14186700), water year 1975.

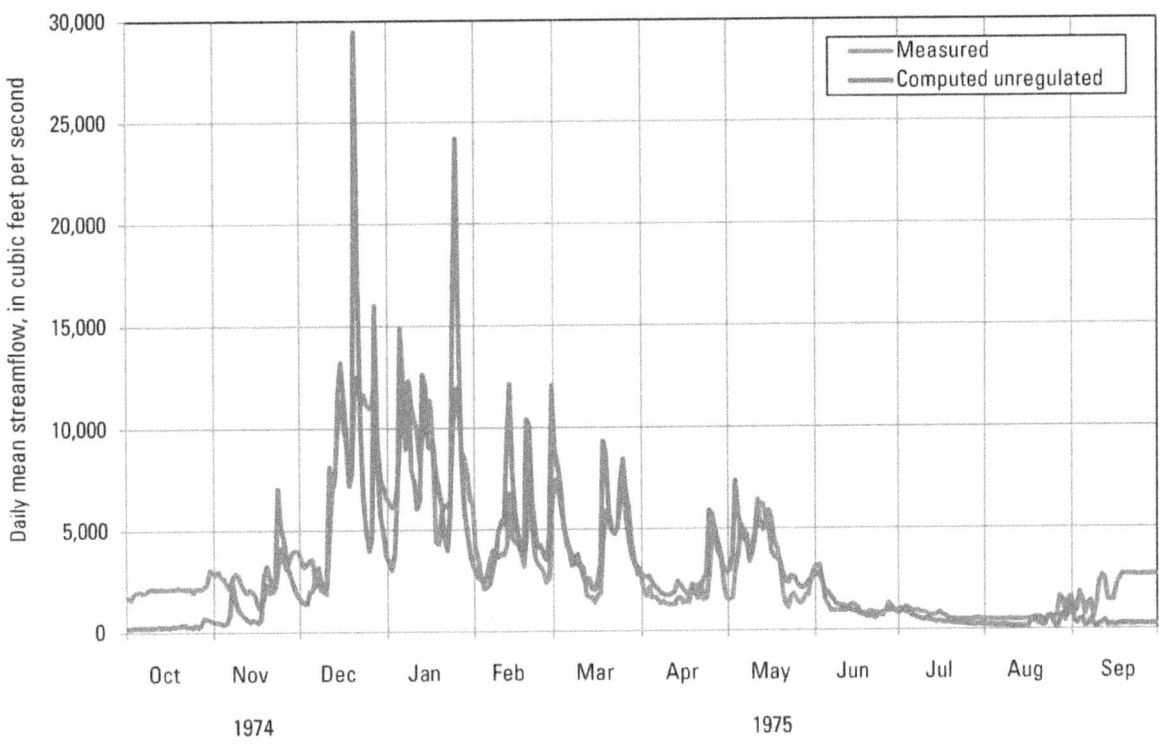

Figure 22. Graph showing daily mean streamflow in Reach 6 at South Santiam River at Waterloo, Oregon (14187500), water year 1975.

Under regulated streamflow conditions for 1967–2009, the median annual 1-day maximum streamflow at the three gages (Middle Santiam River at mouth near Foster [14186500], South Santiam River at Foster [14186700], and South Santiam River at Waterloo [14187500]) decreased by 39 to 52 percent in comparison to computed unregulated streamflow conditions (table 9). In contrast, the median of annual 7-day minimum streamflows increased by 310 to 335 percent at Foster (14186700) and Waterloo (14187500) gages, respectively (table 10). Both those gages are downstream from Foster Dam. However, for the gage below Green Peter Dam (Middle Santiam River at mouth near Foster [14186500]), the median annual 7-day minimum streamflow decreased by 39 percent. Summer low flows commonly increased as a result of dam regulation. The decrease in low flows for the Reach 4 gage below Green Peter Dam may have been because of an error in the regulated stream-flow time series. The 1967–2009 regulated streamflow time series for this station was entire-ly computed because the gage was discontinued in 1966. The time series, provided by USACE,

was compiled from reservoir modeling output and contained many consecutive days of exactly 50 ft^3/s of discharge.

The median monthly streamflows at the three Reach 4–6 gages (Middle Santiam River at mouth near Foster [14186500], South Santiam River at Foster [14186700], and South Santiam River at Waterloo [14187500]) decreased in the late win-ter and spring (February–May) and increased from summer to winter (July–January) as a result of dam regulation (table 11).

For the two gages below Foster Dam, South Santiam at Foster (14186700) and at Waterloo (14187500), the 5-percent streamflow exceedance increased slightly (less than 5 percent) under reg-ulation (figs. 23–25; table 12). The 95-percent streamflow exceedance increased 266 and 283 percent for gages 14186700 and 14187500, re-spectively. However, the 95-percent streamflow exceedance for the gage below Green Peter Dam (14186500) decreased by 46 percent, possibly because of an error in the computed streamflow time series as previously mentioned.

37

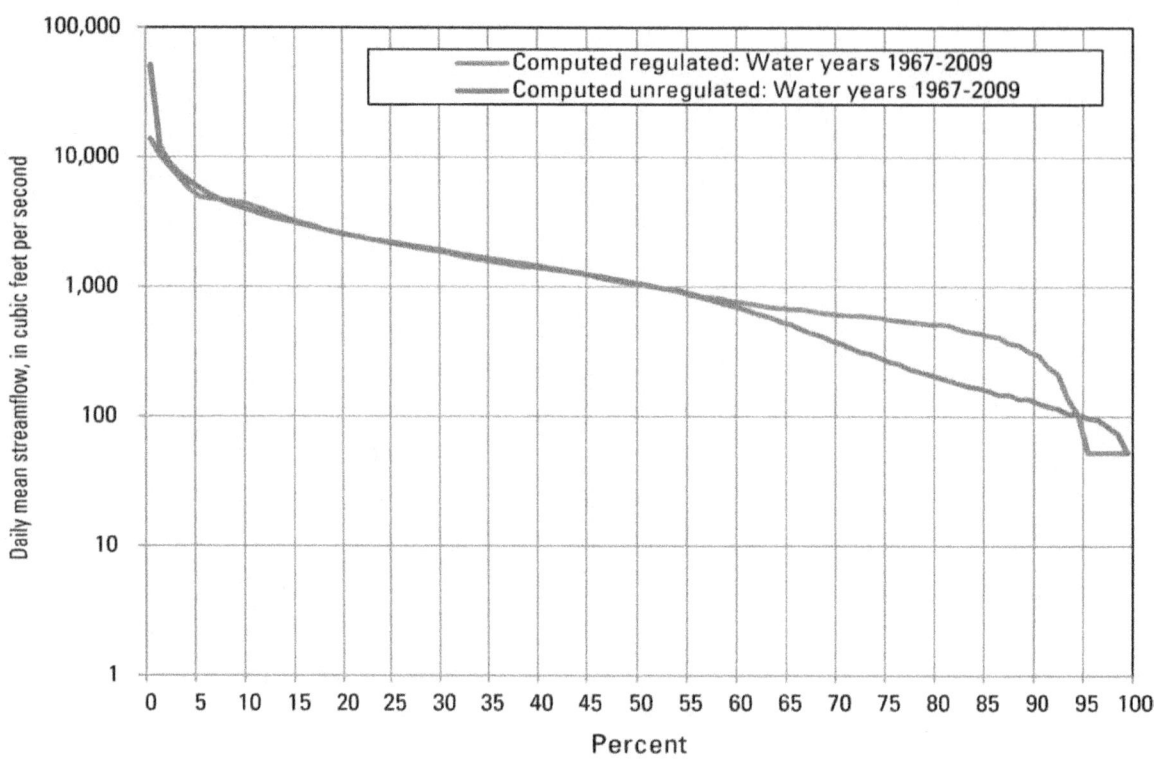

Figure 23. Graph showing percent of daily mean streamflows equaled or exceeded in Reach 4 at Middle Santiam River at mouth near Foster, Oregon (14186500), water years 1967–2009.

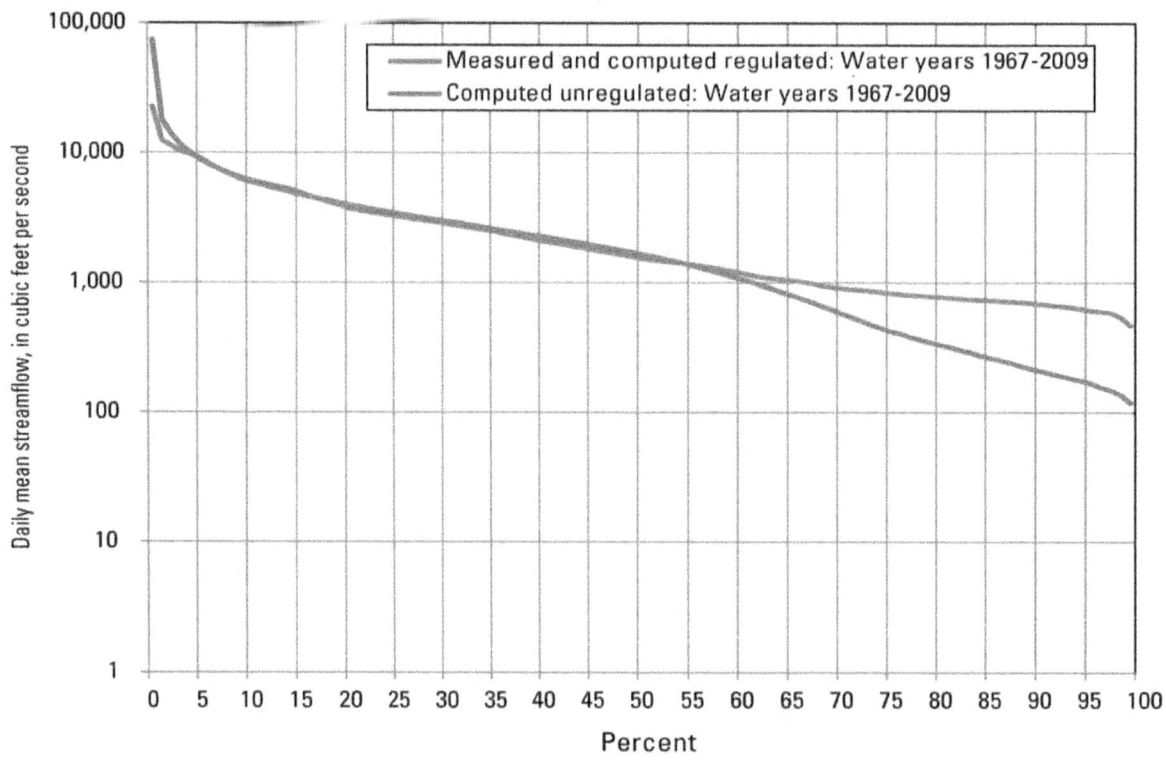

Figure 24. Graph showing percent of daily mean streamflows equaled or exceeded in Reach 5 at South Santiam River at Foster, Oregon (14186700), water years 1967–2009.

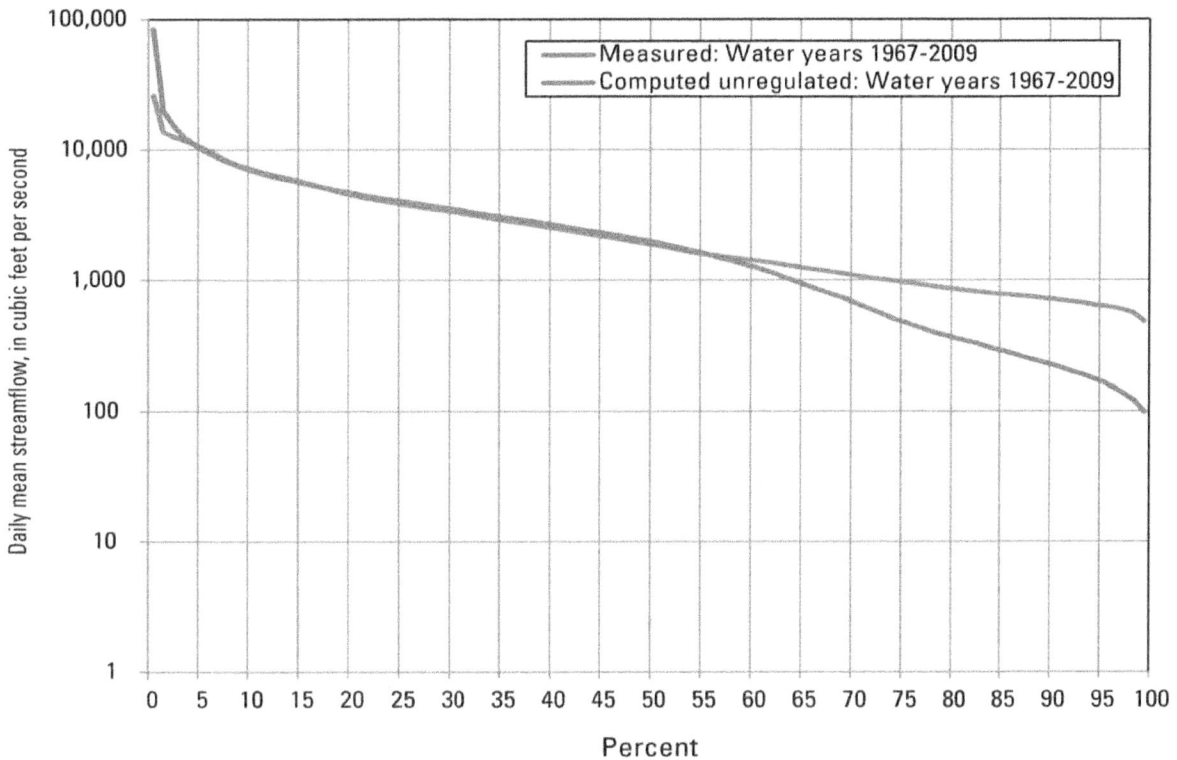

Figure 25. Graph showing percent of daily mean streamflows equaled or exceeded in Reach 6 at South Santiam River at Waterloo, Oregon (14187500), water years 1967–2009.

Main-Stem Santiam River

The Santiam River at Jefferson (14189000) gage began continuous operation in water year 1940 and is downstream from all four USACE dams (Detroit, Big Cliff, Green Peter, and Foster) (fig. 26). Although the effect of the four dams is evident in this streamflow record, the effect is less than the effect seen in the streamflow data in the North and South Santiam River basins because those gages are closer to the dams. In addition to the greater travel time, the effect of the dams is also decreased at the Jefferson (14189000) gage because of substantial natural inflow between the dams and the station.

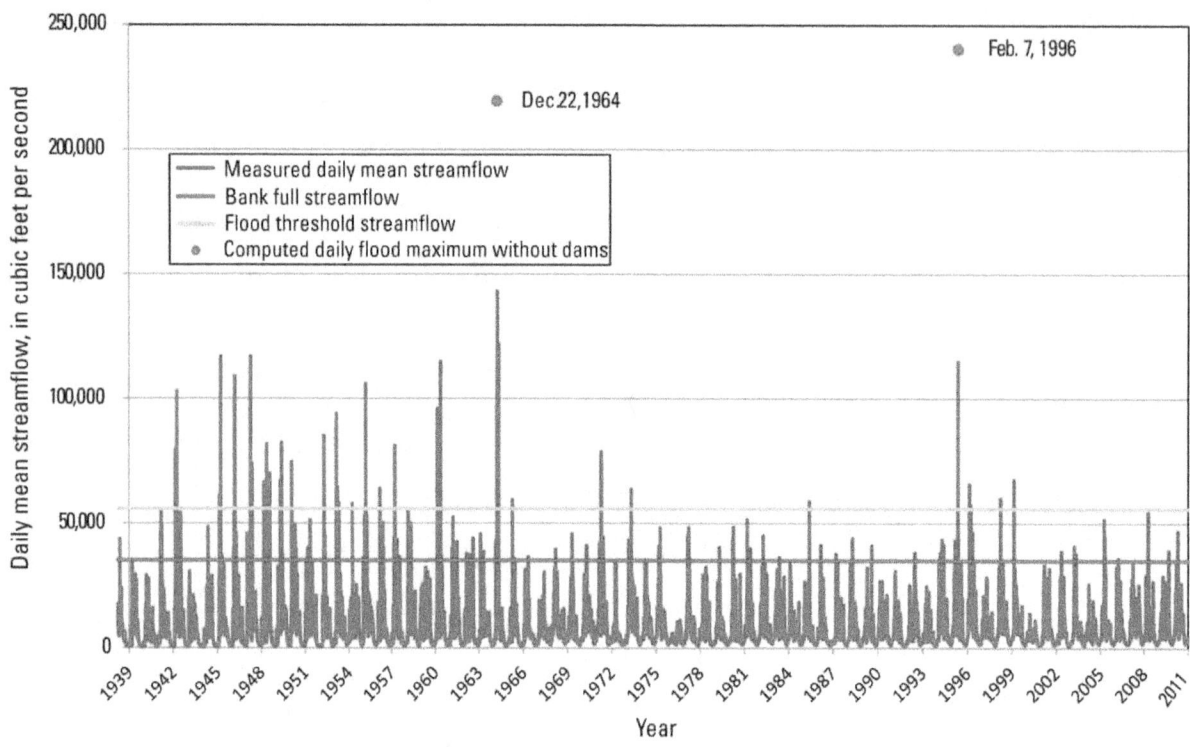

Figure 26. Graph showing daily mean streamflow in Reach 7 at Santiam River at Jefferson, Oregon (14189000), water years 1940–2011.

Prior to construction of the North Santiam River dams in 1953, daily mean streamflow exceeded the USACE defined bankfull and flood threshold discharges on average 7.46 and 1.92 times per year, respectively. During water years 1953–2011, daily mean streamflow exceeded bankfull and flood threshold discharges on average 4.12 and 0.66 times per year, respectively. The largest flood events in the post-dam regulation period were 143,000 ft^3/s (December 23, 1964) and 115,000 ft^3/s (February 7, 1996). If the dams had not been constructed, the USACE estimated that these two events would have been 219,000 ft^3/s (December 22, 1964) and 240,000 ft^3/s (February 7, 1996) (fig. 26). The full effect of flood control does not appear until water year 1967 when the South Santiam dams were completed. Although it may appear that the North Santiam River dams provide less flood control than the South Santiam River dams, it should be noted that the late 1950s and early 1960s (before construction of the South Santiam River dams)

was a wet period. The effect of flood control in the North and South Santiam Rivers likely is comparable because the drainage area above Foster Dam (492 mi^2) is comparable to the drainage area above Big Cliff Dam (449 mi^2). Also, at their confluence, the drainage areas of the North and South Santiam Rivers are 1,770 and 1,810 mi^2, respectively.

Using annual peak flows, which have been measured at the Jefferson (14189000) gage starting in 1908, flood frequencies were separately computed for the pre-dam (1908–1952) and post-dam (1953–2010) periods. As a result of dam regulation, the 1.5-, 10-, 50-, 100-, and 500-year peak flows decreased by 29 to 33 percent (table 8). This is substantially less than the peak-flow decreases computed for the gages in the North and South Santiam River basins because those gages are upstream closer to the dams.

Similar to the North and South Santiam River gages, a comparison of measured and computed unregulated mean daily streamflows (water

40

years 1953–2009) at the Jefferson (14189000) gage showed that February–May streamflows decreased and July–November streamflows increased under regulated streamflow conditions (fig. 27). Because the Jefferson (14189000) gage is farther downstream from the dams, the effect of streamflow regulation caused by the dams is less pronounced than at the upstream gages.

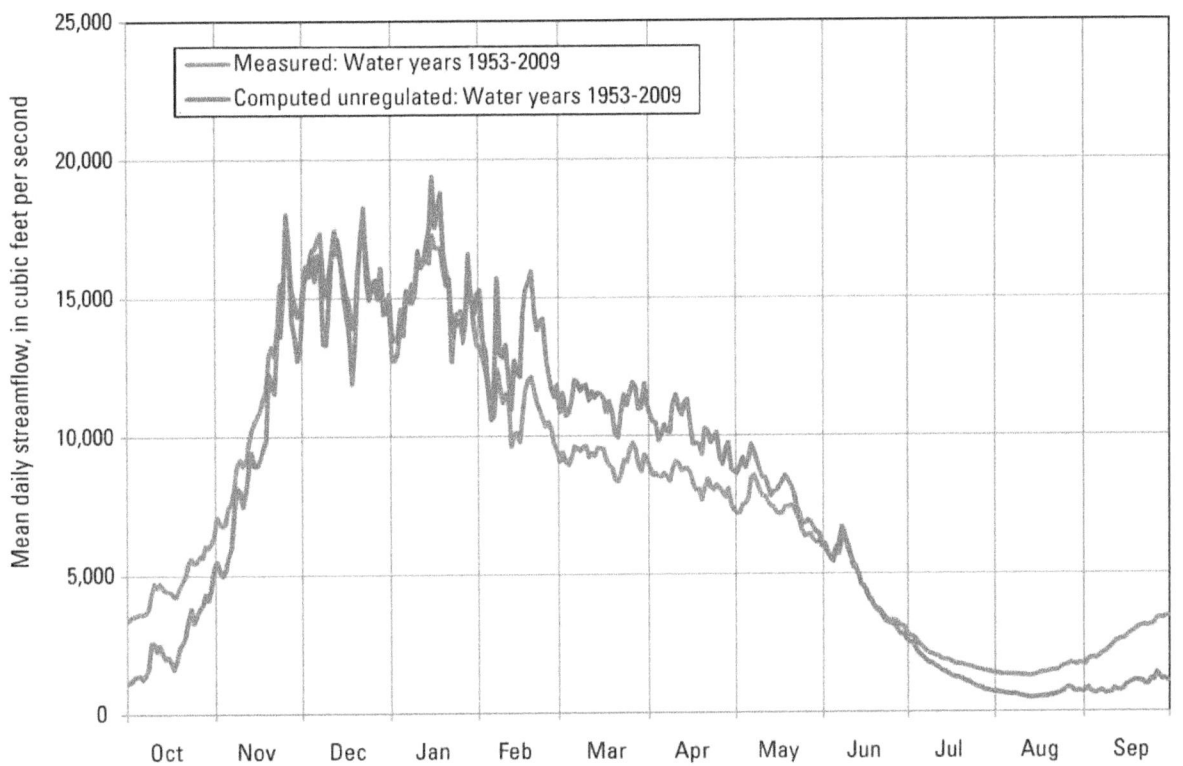

Figure 27. Graph showing mean daily streamflow in Reach 7 at Santiam River at Jefferson, Oregon (14189000), water years 1953–2009.

A comparison of measured regulated and computed unregulated daily mean streamflows at the Jefferson (14189000) gage during a single average hydrologic year (1975) showed the effects of dam regulation (fig. 28). Flood peaks were reduced in magnitude and streamflows were higher in September and October. The day-to-day dam operation that is noticeable in the hydrographs for North Santiam River at Niagara (14181500) and Middle Santiam River near Foster (14186500), which are both immediately downstream from Big Cliff and Green Peter Dams, respectively, does not appear in the Jefferson (14189000) hydrograph.

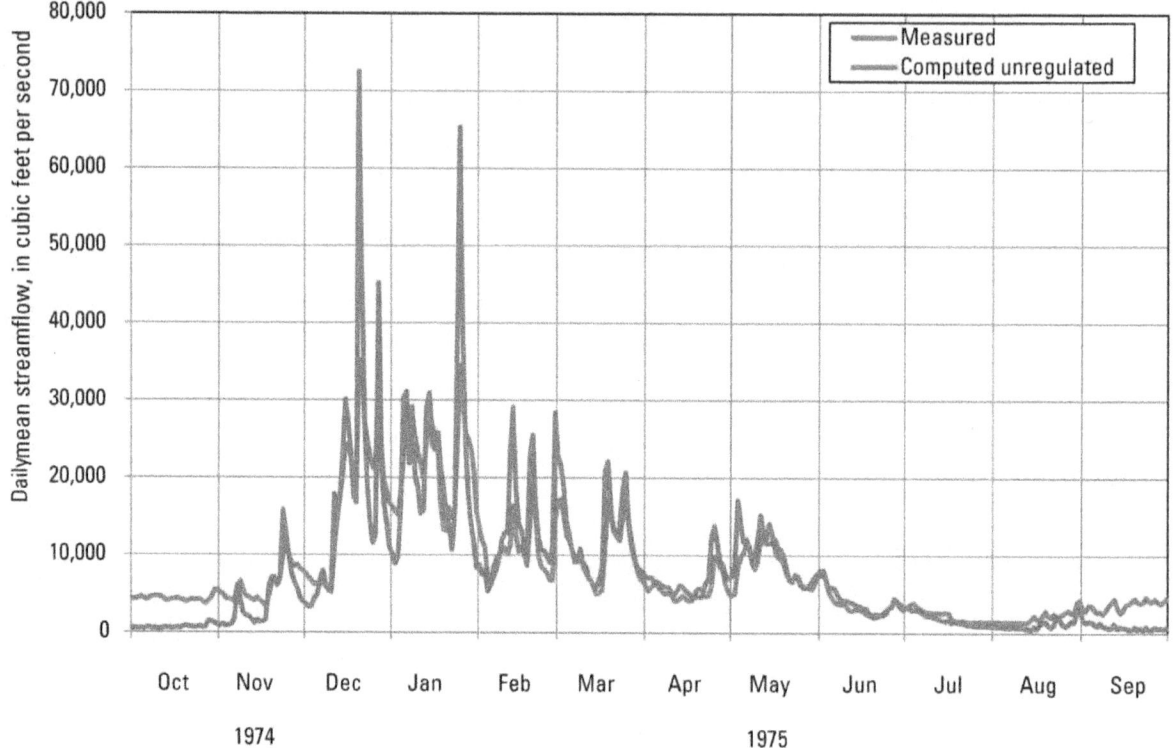

Figure 28. Graph showing daily mean streamflow in Reach 7 at Santiam River at Jefferson, Oregon (14189000), water year 1975.

Under regulated streamflow conditions from 1953 to 2009, the median of annual 1-day maximum streamflows at the Jefferson (14189000) gage decreased by 39 percent (table 9). However, the median of annual 7-day minimum streamflows increased by 237 percent (table 10). The median monthly streamflows were consistent with the median monthly streamflows at the six upstream gages (Reaches 1–6). Monthly streamflows at the Jefferson (14189000) gage decreased in the late winter and spring (February–May) and increased in the summer to early winter (June–January) as a result of dam regulation (table 11). The 5-percent streamflow exceedance increased slightly (less than 5 percent), whereas the 95-percent streamflow exceedance increased by 211 percent (fig. 29, table 12).

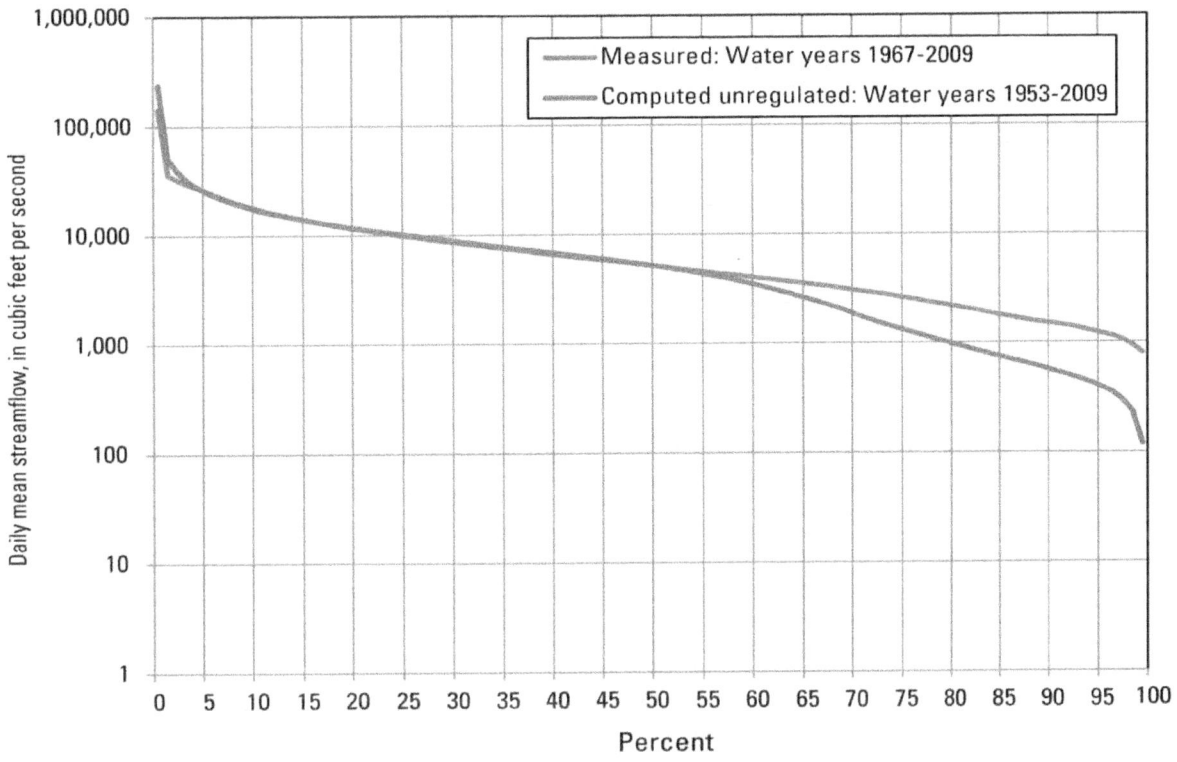

Figure 29. Graph showing percent of daily mean streamflows equaled or exceeded in Reach 7 at Santiam River at Jefferson, Oregon (14189000), water years 1953–2009.

Geomorphic and Ecological Synopsis

This section provides a brief assessment of geomorphic and ecological characteristics within the Santiam River basin and their responses to streamflow. The findings from this assessment are based primarily on qualitative observations and simple measurements drawn from existing datasets and a review of prior relevant studies. Because a comprehensive spatially explicit study of terrestrial and aquatic habitats and species of concern is lacking for the Santiam River basin, this study used information from Gregory and others (2007a, 2007b) that provided a broad summary of species and habitats for the Willamette River basin. Other datasets used in this Santiam assessment include U.S. Department of Agriculture National Agriculture Imagery Program (NAIP) 2009 digital orthophotographs (1-m resolution); a Quaternary geology map (O'Connor and others, 2001); locations of USACE revetments (Jerry Otto, U.S. Army Corps of Engineers, written commun., Jan 13, 2012); and a land-cover map from 1850 (Gregory and others, 2002a). General summary reports including the Willamette Project Biological Opinions

(National Marine Fisheries Service, 2008; U.S. Fish and Wildlife Service, 2008), Biological Assessment (U.S. Army Corps of Engineers, 2007), and watershed assessments (E and S Environmental Chemistry Inc., 2002; E and S Environmental Chemistry Inc. and South Santiam Watershed Council, 2000) also were used. Previous studies of historical channel change in the Santiam River basin (Fletcher and Davidson, 1988; Klingeman, 1973), as well as other nearby basins, including the Willamette (Wallick and others, 2006, 2007), Middle and Coast Fork (Gregory and others, 2002a, 2002b) and McKenzie River basins (Risley and others, 2010a, 2010b) also were incorporated in this study.

Geomorphic Characteristics of Study Reaches

In the following section, geomorphic characteristics of the North, South, and main-stem Santiam Rivers are briefly summarized and displayed. More complete descriptions for each reach are provided in Appendix D. Although the Middle Santiam River (Reach 4) is listed in Appendix C, it is not described in this section because it has limited habitat potential owing to releases from the upstream Green Peter Dam that likely scour the channel in the upper portion of the reach and because the lower portion of the reach is under constant inundation by the downstream Foster Lake reservoir.

North Santiam River Channel Morphology

The upper 2.8 mi of Reach 1 is bounded by Detroit and Big Cliff Dams. Downstream from the dams, the North Santiam River transitions from a narrow channel confined by steep bedrock valley walls to a broad, alluvial river with numerous side channels and gravel bars before joining the South Santiam River near Jefferson. Between Big Cliff Dam (RM 58.1) and the USGS gage at Niagara (14181500) (RM 57.3), the North Santiam River flows predominantly over bedrock and coarse bed material through a narrow canyon with few gravel bars. Downstream from the bedrock rapids near the town of Niagara (RM 55.0), the flood plain widens to about 0.6 mi, and active gravel bars begin to appear, though they are small (2,000–3,000 yds^2) and typically more than a mile apart (fig. 30). There are several large (up to 16,000 yd^2) densely vegetated mid-channel bars near the downstream end of Reach 1 near the Little North Santiam River confluence. Channel and flood-plain confinement owing primarily to basin topography throughout Reach 1 limit channel complexity and flood-plain processes; however, small, relict secondary channel features such as those between RM 40 and RM 44 may provide off-channel habitat at high flows.

Base from 2009 U.S. Department of Agriculture
aerial photography, 1-meter resolution.
Universal Transverse Mercator Projection, Zone 10.
North American Datum of 1983

N

EXPLANATION
⊙   Approximate river miles

Figure 30. Aerial photograph showing channel and flood-plain morphology in study Reach 1 of the Santiam River basin, Oregon, on the North Santiam River.

Downstream from the Little North Santiam River, the flood plain of the North Santiam River along Reach 2 widens from 0.2 mi to nearly 1.5 mi as the channel adopts an increasingly complex, multi-threaded morphology (fig. 31). Just below the upstream boundary of Reach 2, the river flows through a short, confined segment where the flood plain is about 0.2 mi wide and is closely flanked by Pleistocene terraces (fig. 31). Within this segment, historical channel change has likely been minimal, and a specific gage analysis by Klingeman (1973) found little indication of aggradation or incision between 1935 and 1965 at the USGS streamflow gage at Mehama (14183000) (RM 38.7). Farther downstream, the North Santiam River below RM 35 flows through a broad flood plain and historically probably displayed an anastomosing planform, meaning the river had multiple converging and diverging channels separated by large, semi-stable islands much like the upper Willamette River above Harrisburg as described in Gregory and others (2002b). Presently, many of the secondary channel features along Reach 2 are densely vegetated, and flow is mainly confined to a single channel, except for RM 26–33, where the active channel is over 0.25 mi wide and accommodates a diverse array of side channels, alcoves, islands, and gravel bars (fig. 31).

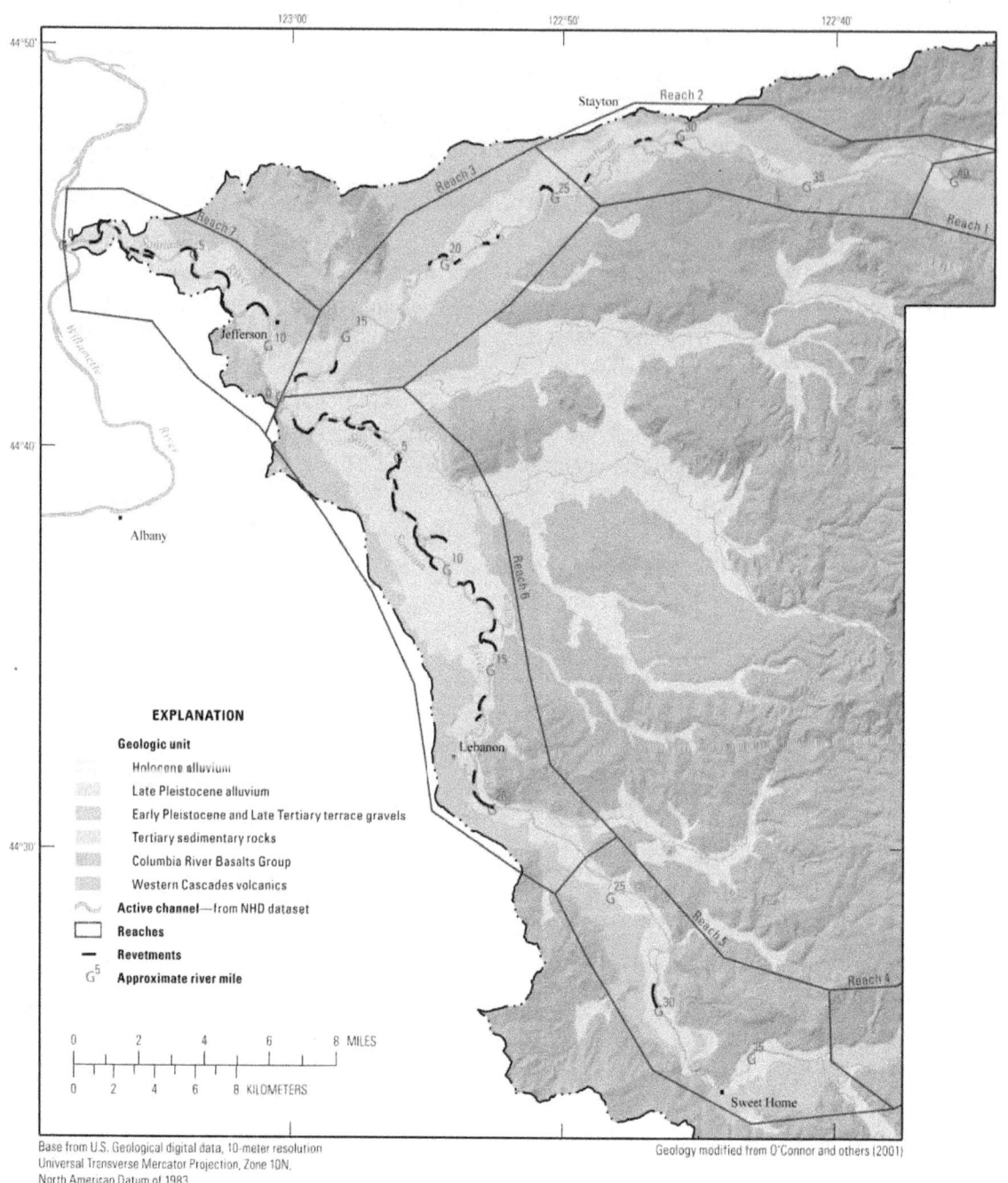

Figure 31. Map showing surficial geology and revetments for alluvial segments of the Santiam River, Oregon, study area. Late Pleistocene alluvium is a combination of units Qff2, Qg1, and Qg2; Holocene alluvium is a combination of units Qalc, Qalf, Qau, and Qbf; all other units shown from O'Connor and others (2001).

Channel complexity increases downstream along North Santiam River through Reach 3. This historically dynamic, multi-channeled reach is flanked by a broad flood plain 0.7–1.5 mi wide (fig. 31). Active gravel bars up to 25,000 yd^2 in area are present throughout the reach and are nearly continuous along the multi-channeled segment near RM 17–21 (fig. 32). While nearly half of Reach 3 presently displays complex, multi-channeled planform, densely vegetated, relict secondary channel and flood-plain features are found throughout the entire reach. An example of a segment in Reach 3 containing modern channel complexity and relict channel features is shown in figure 32. Because there is little revetment along the North Santiam River in Reaches 2 and 3 (fig. 31), channel processes including meander migration, bar growth and creation, and maintenance of secondary channel features are mainly determined by the flow and coarse-sediment regimes. These processes have been altered by upstream dams.

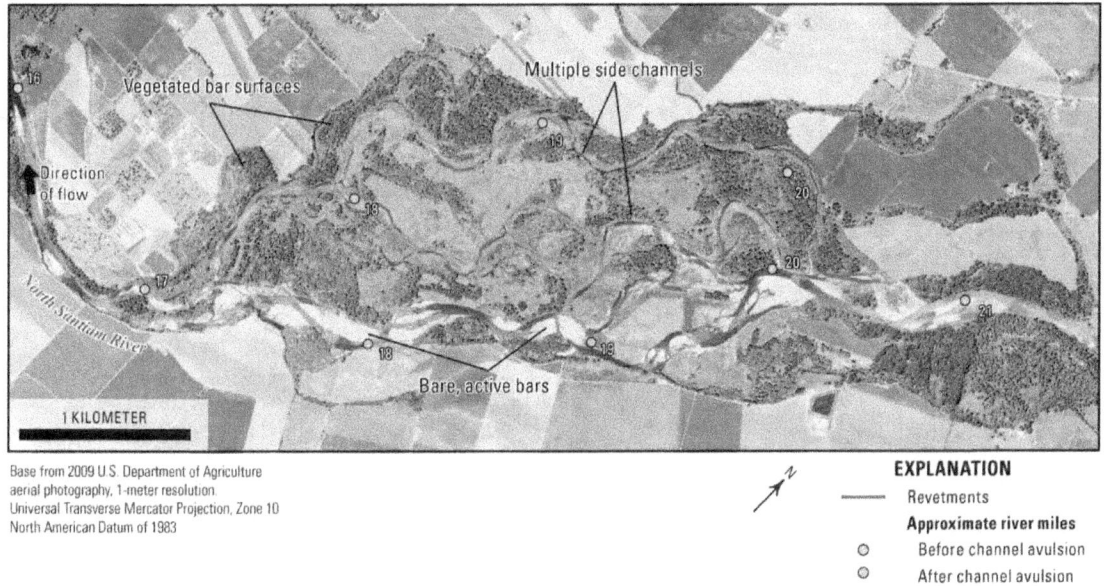

Figure 32. Aerial photograph showing channel and flood-plain morphology in study Reach 3 of the Santiam River basin, Oregon, on the North Santiam River.

South Santiam River Channel Morphology

Historically, the lower South Santiam River between RM 0 and RM 18 along Reach 6 likely displayed a complex, anastomosing planform. Presently, this segment, as well as Reach 5 (14.7 mi of channel below Foster Dam), primarily occupies a low-sinuosity, single-thread channel (fig. 31). Although the flood plain in Reach 5 varies from 0.1 mi wide near Sweet Home to nearly 1 mi wide elsewhere, much of the channel flows against naturally occurring hard surfaces including the flood-plain margin and basalt underlying the valley walls that limits channel complexity and provides stability (fig. 3). A specific gage analysis at the USGS gage at Waterloo (14187500) (RM 23.3) near the boundary between Reach 5 and Reach 6 indicates minimal change in bed elevation between 1935 and 1965 (Klingeman, 1973) underscoring the overall stability of this segment of the South Santiam River. There is only one area with moderate channel complexity along Reach 5 (between RM 28 and RM 29) where the river is flanked on both sides by Holocene alluvium and has multiple channels. Active gravel bars are sparse throughout Reach 5 and are relatively small (less than 1,500 yd^2). The reach has a number of densely vegetated bar surfaces such as the island at RM 36 (fig. 33).

Base from 2009 U.S. Department of Agriculture
aerial photography, 1-meter resolution.
Universal Transverse Mercator Projection, Zone 10
North American Datum of 1983

N

EXPLANATION

○   Approximate river miles

Figure 33. Aerial photograph showing channel and flood-plain morphology in study Reach 5 of the Santiam River basin, Oregon, on the South Santiam River.

The South Santiam River along Reach 6 can be divided into two distinct segments. From RM 18 (Lebanon) to its confluence with the North Santiam River, the river flows through a broad Holocene flood plain 1.75–3 mi wide that historically had a dynamic, multi-thread channel. Upstream between RM 18 and RM 23, the river flowed through a relatively narrow flood plain (0.2–0.8 mi wide) that historically supported a more stable, single-thread channel (fig. 31). Although the channel in the lower segment (RM 0–18) is flanked on both sides by easily erodible Holocene alluvium and was historically prone to rapid meander migration, much of the reach is presently stabilized by revetments constructed in the mid-to-late 20th century (fig. 31). Bank stabilization in combination with construction of the Foster and Big Cliff Dams resulted in substantial reductions in channel complexity and gravel-bar area. For example, Fletcher and Davidson (1988) reported a 56-percent reduction in the area of gravel bars between 1936 and 1981. The 2009 orthophotographs show numerous bare, active gravel bars up to 25,000 yd^2, downstream from RM 18 in areas lacking bank revetment (for example, RM 4.5 in fig. 34). Gravel bars and channel complexity is much less where one or both banks are stabilized with revetment (Fletcher and Davidson, 1988; as depicted between RM 5 and RM 6 in fig. 34). Downstream from RM 18, extensive formerly active bar surfaces and relic secondary channel features are presently stabilized with dense vegetation (for example, RM 5–7 in fig. 34).

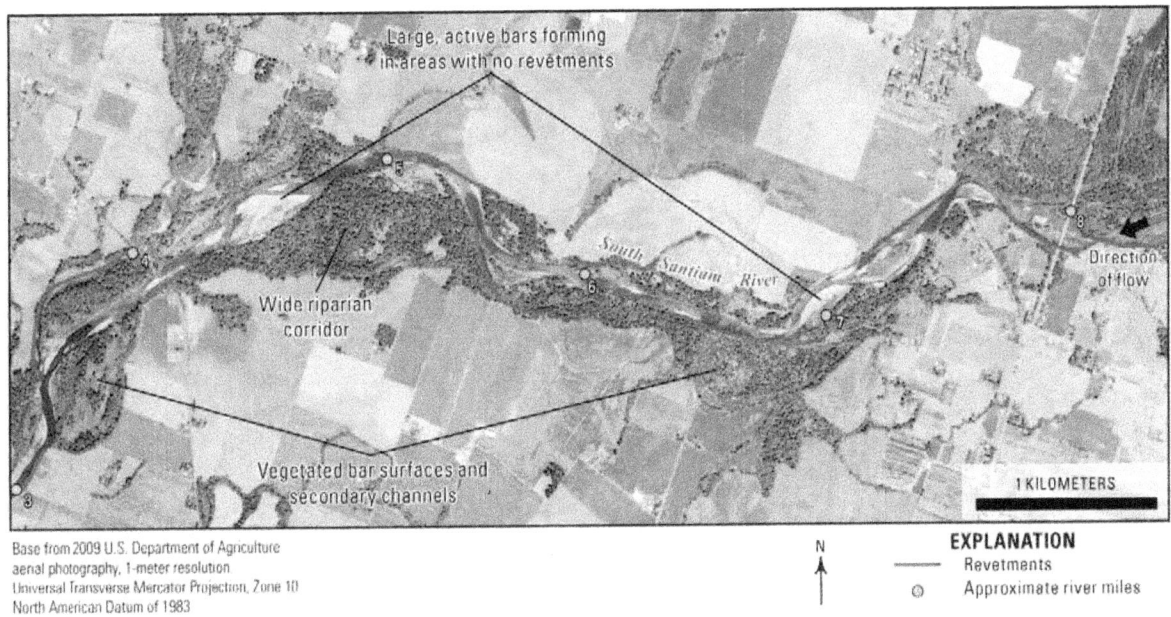

Large, active bars forming in areas with no revetments

South Santiam River

Direction of flow

Wide riparian corridor

Vegetated bar surfaces and secondary channels

1 KILOMETERS

Base from 2009 U.S. Department of Agriculture aerial photography, 1-meter resolution.
Universal Transverse Mercator Projection, Zone 10
North American Datum of 1983

N

EXPLANATION
——— Revetments
○ Approximate river miles

Figure 34. Aerial photograph showing channel and flood-plain morphology in study Reach 6 of the Santiam River basin, Oregon, on the South Santiam River.

Main-Stem Santiam River Channel Morphology

The main-stem Santiam River below the confluence of the North and South Santiam Rivers historically formed dynamic multi-thread channels that were prone to rapid meander migration and avulsion prior to flood control and bank protection. Presently, the Santiam River along Reach 7 is mainly confined to a single channel (fig. 31) with several sections where flow is split by mid-channel bars (for example, RM 5.3 in fig. 35). Although Reach 7 flows through a broad flood plain that ranges up to 3 mi wide, revetment currently flanks much of the channel, restricting bank erosion, channel complexity, and bar growth (fig. 31). Between the confluence of the South and North Santiam Rivers and RM 10, the channel is confined by sedimentary rocks (fig. 31). Large, bare, active gravel bars are intermittent but can exceed 100,000 yd^2, especially in the lower 5 mi of Reach 7 near its confluence with the Willamette River (fig. 35). Throughout the reach, there are many relict bar surfaces and secondary channel features that presently have dense vegetative cover. However, these features may be activated during exceptionally high flows (fig. 35).

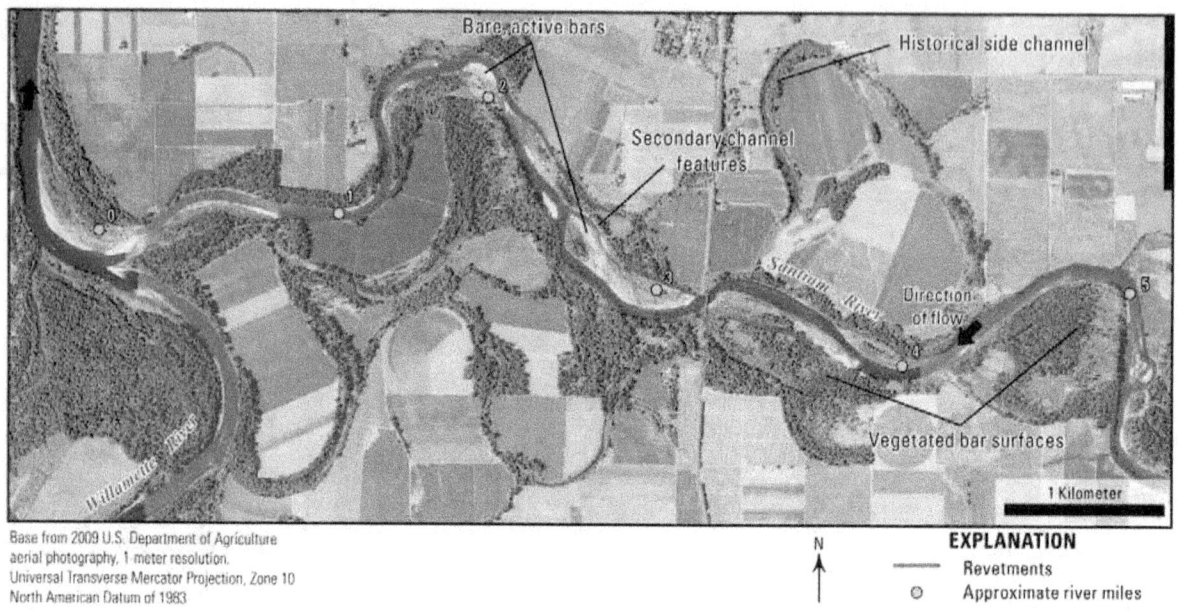

Base from 2009 U.S. Department of Agriculture
aerial photography, 1-meter resolution.
Universal Transverse Mercator Projection, Zone 10
North American Datum of 1983

N

Figure 35. Aerial photograph showing channel and flood-plain morphology in study Reach 7 of the Santiam River basin, Oregon, Santiam River main stem.

Specific gage analyses at the USGS gage at Jefferson (14189000) (RM 9.6) for the period 1941–1986 shows substantial (greater than 1 ft) erosion from 1941 to 1964 (Klingeman, 1973) and then relatively stable channel conditions from 1964 to 1986 (Fletcher and Davidson, 1988). Fletcher and Davidson (1988) attribute these overall changes to initial scouring of alluvial deposits and later cross-section control by an exposed bedrock outcrop slightly downstream. This bedrock outcrop is probably a remnant from the adjacent Pleistocene terraces composed of partially cemented gravels (unit Qg1) (fig. 31), which can form resistant shoals and riffles (Wallick and others, 2006). Therefore, the specific gage analysis for the Jefferson gage may not be representative of other locations in this reach because the bank materials here are not the easily erodible Holocene alluvium found elsewhere along this reach.

Terrestrial and Aquatic Habitats and Key Species

Geomorphic processes in response to streamflow are critical for creating and maintaining aquatic and terrestrial habitat. A few examples of ecological responses to geomorphic and hydrologic processes can include (1) fish spawning in gravel substrates created from flooding; (2) fish migration and spawning in response to minimum streamflows and cooler stream temperatures; or (3) cottonwood seed dispersal in response to fresh bare ground exposure caused by flood scouring. The Santiam River basin historically provided diverse habitats that supported many aquatic and terrestrial ecosystems. Many of these habitats have been substantially altered by modifications in the river's flow and sediment transport or are inaccessible because of passage issues at dams and culverts. Gregory and others (2007a, 2007b) and Risley and others (2010a) provide detailed synopses of aquatic and terrestrial species likely to be affected by flow modifications in the Middle and Coast Fork Willamette and McKenzie River drainages. A brief summary of key ecological species and habitat needs are outlined below and are provided by reach in Appendix D.

The multi-channel segments with off-channel and secondary features along the North Santiam River below RM 33 and the main-stem Santiam River below RM 7 provide off-channel and backwater habitats critical for species such as Oregon chub, red legged frog, and western pond turtle (Gregory and others, 2007a, 2007b). These segments also have secondary channel features and sloughs that provide high-flow refugia and rearing habitat for native fish, including spring Chinook and winter steelhead. Although these features are present on the South Santiam River below RM 18, they are much less extensive because of revetments and channel simplification than on the North Santiam River. Other native fish species that use the North, South, and main-stem Santiam Rivers include rainbow trout, cutthroat trout, northern pike minnow, sand rollers, shiners, sculpins, and dace (Gregory and others, 2007a, 2007b).

The broad, low-gradient flood plains of the Santiam River historically contained a complex mosaic of riparian forests and wetlands, which has been simplified throughout the study area since the 1850s. Presently, the riparian forest corridor is nearly contiguous along lower North Santiam River below RM 33, the South Santiam River below RM 18, and the main-stem Santiam River below RM 7. Within these sections, the forest corridor ranges in width from a narrow band of trees to more than 0.7 mi (as shown in figs. 32, 34, and 35) and likely includes tree species such as black cottonwood, riparian willows, and white alder (Gregory and others, 2007a, 2007b). These species are associated with the more dynamic multi-channel stretches because they depend on high flows in winter and spring for seed dispersal, active sediment transport and deposition to create exposed fine sediment patches for germination, and erosion to remove canopy cover that otherwise may preclude establishment.

Potential Geomorphic and Ecological Response to Environmental Flow Releases

No comprehensive study relating streamflow with specific geomorphic or ecological responses exists for the Santiam River basin. Hence, the following section discusses possible effects of environmental flow releases on physical habitat and riparian ecosystems based on known relations between channel processes and flow and

sediment regimes and previous environmental flow studies in the Willamette River basin.

With a wide active channel, abundance of gravel bars and secondary channel features, and limited revetments, the lower North Santiam River below RM 33 would likely respond dynamically to environmental flow releases. Channel and flood-plain response to high-flow releases (including high-flow pulses and small and large floods) may include meander migration and possibly avulsions at very high discharges. Bank erosion from meander migration and avulsions would likely supply coarse bed-material sediment for deposition downstream, forming gravel bars, riffles, pools, and spawning habitats. Bank erosion along forested portions of the flood plain could introduce large wood into the active channel, providing cover and habitat complexity for fish, amphibians, and mammals and possible blockages that support further bar growth and pool formation. High flows may also support the maintenance and creation of secondary channel features; scour stabilizing vegetation from relict gravel bars depending on flow magnitude; and assist with seed dispersal, organic matter exchange between the river and riparian areas, and deposition of sediment suitable for seedling germinations.

Reaches lined by revetment or naturally occurring material resistive to erosion may have more limited responses to flow modifications. For instance, Reach 6 of the South Santiam below RM 18 has extensive revetment that limits bank erosion, recruitment of gravel and large wood from the flood plain, and creation of new habitats suitable to riparian vegetation establishment. Because revetments have also restricted lateral migration and limited bar growth along the South Santiam River (Fletcher and Davidson, 1988), environmental flow releases on the South Santiam may not be as effective at increasing bar area and spawning habitat as they might be on the lower North Santiam River, which has fewer revetments. Other areas unlikely to display dynamic channel response to environmental flow releases include the stable semiconsolidated gravel and bedrock dominated segments of the study area including the North Santiam River (Reaches 1 and 2) above RM 33 and the South Santiam River above RM 18 (Reaches 4, 5, and 6).

Another important consideration of environmental flow releases is the possibility of channel incision and bed coarsening in response to high flows caused by sediment trapping behind the dams. The dams on the North and South Santiam Rivers trap sediment from 59 and 47 percent of these basins, respectively. The beds of downstream reaches have likely coarsened in response to excess transport capacity because dams limit sediment supply (National Marine Fisheries Service, 2008; Fletcher and Davidson, 1988). Therefore, it is possible that high-flow releases may further coarsen the bed or trigger bed-level lowering, especially along alluvial segments where there are limited upstream sources of bed material from tributaries or bank erosion. Further assessment of the influence of environmental flow releases on bed coarsening and channel lowering would entail development of a bed-material budget along with a comprehensive analysis of historical changes in grain size and bed elevations.

In addition to modifying physical habitat, streamflow also affects the spawning, rearing, and migration behavior of fish species. Discharge during autumn increased throughout the study area, which coincides with late summer and early autumn spawning by spring Chinook and is followed by lower than historical flows during the late winter (table 11). Such flood-control operations in late winter may lead to dewatering of salmon redds and could potentially kill incubating eggs and alevins (Reiser and White, 1983). Additionally, stream-temperature regimes have been modified by flow regulations, causing temperatures to be cooler in summer and warmer in autumn (Rounds, 2010). Changes to the thermal regime can have a direct impact on salmonid outmigrations in winter and spawning and incubation in fall (Gregory and others, 2007a, 2007b). Reach 5 of the South Santiam River between RM 30 and RM 35 may be especially sensitive to such

flow and, probably, stream-temperature fluctuations because spawning of spring Chinook salmon is especially heavy in this area (National Marine Fisheries Service, 2008, section 4.5). Relations between life history and monthly streamflow and stream temperature similar to those developed for the Middle and Coast Fork Willamette and McKenzie Rivers (Gregory and others, 2007a, 2007b; Risley and others, 2010a) could assist in developing basin-specific environmental flow releases for the Santiam River basin.

Streamflow patterns also influence other aquatic and riparian species. For example, extreme low-flow periods, which can be exacerbated by withdrawals, can lower groundwater levels and threaten the survival of riparian seedlings such as black cottonwood and white alder (Gregory and others, 2007a, 2007b). In contrast, large floods may erode young trees on low-lying floodplain surfaces, but they can also disperse seeds and stems and deposit fresh sediment patches at lower elevations within the active channel, where new seedlings can germinate, ultimately increasing the diversity and age classes of riparian vegetation (Gregory and others, 2007a, 2007b). To assist in the development of environmental flow releases that aim to increase the diversity and age classes of native riparian forests, relations between streamflow and riparian vegetation could be created for the Santiam River basin similar to those developed for the Middle and Coast Fork Willamette and McKenzie River basins (Gregory and others, 2007a, 2007b; Risley and others, 2010a).

Future Studies

This study provides a framework and baseline information for developing environmental flow guidelines in the Santiam River basin. Central to a sound environmental flow program is establishing robust, quantitative relations between streamflow, channel and flood-plain processes, and ecosystem response. These relations can be quantified by (1) understanding existing channel and flood-plain processes (post-dam, post-revetment) along lower, alluvial reaches, (2) understanding relations between environmental flows and terrestrial and aquatic habitats and species, and (3) documenting existing conditions and those following environmental flow releases of different magnitudes. Such information would provide a solid basis for evaluating future hydrologic, geomorphic, and ecological changes and comprehensive adaptive management in the Santiam River basin. To address the three objectives above, it will be necessary to evaluate streamflow data and analyses, bed-load material transport rates and sediment budget, channel and flood-plain morphology, and terrestrial and aquatic responses to environmental flows.

Streamflow Data and Analysis

Modeling and predicting channel and habitat response to environmental flow releases requires streamflow information, particularly for peak flows, when bed-material transport, bank erosion, and off-channel habitat creation occurs. Although there is currently a good network of gages throughout the Santiam River basin, additional streamflow and stage monitoring (both continuous and partial-record) are needed in high-priority, multi-thread reaches to relate geomorphic processes (such as flood-plain inundation and scouring of secondary channels) with streamflow. Streamflow data can be tied with ecological information, such as hydrologic connectivity between main-stem and off-channel habitats during high flows and flow recession, to better assess the specific impacts of environmental flow releases on habitat availability to target species.

In addition to new data collection, one- or two-dimensional hydraulic modeling can be used to estimate water-surface elevations during low-flow conditions in reaches that are affected by surface-water withdrawals and possible dam operations. This type of modeling can predict habitat loss caused by the dewatering of side channels and alcoves in alluvial flood plains.

Bed-Material Transport Rates and Sediment Budget

A sediment budget for the Santiam River basin would help assess the effects of environmental flow releases on channel erosion and aggradation, which affect the quality of terrestrial and aquatic habitats. The budget would focus on estimates and (or) measurements of bed-load transport, which carries gravel and other material that build and maintain spawning habitats, gravel bars, and other low-elevation features within the active channel. By comparing the volumes of gravel exiting the Santiam River basin to the volume of gravel delivered to the study area and the volume released through bank erosion, future channel change under different flow and sediment-release scenarios can be evaluated.

Because sediment budgets rely on sediment transport rates, which are difficult to measure, an approach for developing a sediment budget might include several of the following methods to estimate sediment transport:

1. Sediment flux estimates based on bed-load transport equations (Wallick and others, 2010, 2011). Bed-load transport equations calculate transport capacity, and because bed-material supply has been substantially reduced by the Santiam River basin dams, most downstream reaches are likely supply limited (meaning the transport capacity of the river exceeds the available supply of sediment). Sediment flux estimates from bed-load transport equations applied to alluvial reaches will likely provide an estimate of maximum plausible transport.

2. Direct measurements of bed-load transport to verify bed-load transport equations and to estimate bed-load fluxes. Ideally, such measurements would be collected near active USGS gages and downstream from potentially gravel-rich tributaries to provide accurate estimates of total bed-material flux into the lower, alluvial reaches.

3. Empirical GIS-based sediment-yield analyses, factoring in sediment production, delivery to the channels, in-channel attrition, and trapping by dams (Wallick and others, 2011).

4. Sediment flux estimates based on mapped changes in bank erosion and bar area over specific temporal intervals (Wallick and others, 2010). Volumetric change in bank erosion and bar area can be calculated by comparing high-resolution topographic data such as LiDAR from two time periods in alluvial reaches. This component can also serve as a basis for monitoring long-term changes in channel and flood-plain conditions.

Detailed Channel and Flood-Plain Morphology Assessment

A detailed assessment of channel morphology in the Santiam River study area is needed to better understand current channel and habitat conditions and predict changes under different environmental flow scenarios. Mapping channel and flood-plain conditions for different time periods using high-resolution aerial photographs could serve as the starting point for more comprehensive temporal analyses of morphological trends. For example, detailed analyses of changes in channel features (for example, bar area and secondary channel features) could be related to patterns of erosion, deposition, and establishment of vegetation. These analyses will require accounting for the uncertainties associated with the mapping protocols and differences in discharge between the aerial photographs.

Terrestrial and Aquatic Responses

To predict ecological response to flow management, knowledge of the relations between streamflow, water temperature, sediment fluxes, and species of concern and available habitats specific to the Santiam River basin is essential. However, at present, only generalized relations developed for the Middle and Coast Fork Willamette River basins (Gregory and others, 2007a, 2007b) and the McKenzie River basin (Risley and others, 2010a) are available for use in neighboring basins. Additionally, developing flow-management strategies to benefit terrestrial and aquatic species and habitats would be further supported by (1) documentation of terrestrial and aquatic conditions representing post-dam streamflow and sediment-transport conditions and the baseline for determining the success of future flow restorations and (2) supplemental assessments before and after environmental flow releases of different magnitudes to assess terrestrial and aquatic responses and to adapt flow releases to meet restoration targets.

Summary

This report provides a baseline assessment of the hydrology, geomorphology, and effect of streamflow on the ecology of the Santiam River, a tributary of the Willamette River in northwestern Oregon. The assessment was made for the Santiam River environmental flow study, which is a collaborative effort of the U.S. Army Corps of Engineers, The Nature Conservancy, and the U.S. Geological Survey (USGS) under auspices of the Sustainable Rivers Project. In 2002, The Nature Conservancy and the U.S. Army Corps of Engineers began the Sustainable Rivers Project for the purpose of modifying dam operations and implementing environmental flow requirements for various river systems around the country. Information from this report can assist water managers and stakeholders in the development of future environmental flow requirements for the Santiam River basin.

The Santiam River basin has an area of 1,810 mi^2; elevations range from 162 ft at the Willamette River confluence to almost 10,500 ft in the Cascade Range. The two main tributaries in the basin are the North and South Santiam Rivers, which join approximately 9 mi upstream from the Willamette River. Higher elevations in the basin are underlain by young, relatively permeable material consisting of High Cascade volcanic rocks and glacial deposits. Middle and lower elevations of the basin contain older, weathered, less permeable volcanic material characteristic of the Western Cascades. The lower reach in the wide unconstrained flood plain near the Willamette confluence is composed of Quaternary alluvium. Downstream reaches of the basin are mostly privately owned and used for agriculture. Approximately 70 percent of the basin is forested. The basin has long, cool, wet winters and warm, dry summers. Average daily maximum and minimum temperatures at Stayton from 1951 to 2011 were 63 and 42°F, respectively.

The U.S. Army Corps of Engineers owns and operates four dams in the Santiam River basin. The Detroit and the Big Cliff Dams, on the North Santiam River, were put into service in 1953. In 1968 the Green Peter and Foster Dams were completed in the South Santiam River basin. The dams are operated to provide flood control, hydropower production, irrigation, water supply, recreation, water-quality improvement, and aquatic habitat. Surface-water withdrawals within the Santiam River basin for municipal water supply and irrigation are made at various locations downstream from the dams. The Lebanon-Santiam Canal diverts approximately 90 ft^3/s from the South Santiam River upstream from Lebanon. The USGS has operated a network of continuous streamflow monitoring throughout the Santiam River basin since the 1920s. The stations with the longest streamflow records are the North Santiam River at Mehama (14183000: 1921–2011) and the South Santiam River at Waterloo (14187500: 1923–2011).

Seven river reaches, each having distinct streamflow, geomorphic, and ecological conditions, were defined for the study area. The North Santiam River was divided into three reaches between Detroit Dam and the confluence with the South Santiam River. The South Santiam River was also divided into three reaches between Green Peter Dam and the North Santiam River confluence. The final reach along the main-stem Santiam River is between the confluence of the North and South Santiam Rivers and the Willamette River confluence.

To assess the effects of dams and withdrawals on the streamflow regime, measured daily mean streamflow and annual peak-flow data were compiled and used to compute statistics that describe regulated and unregulated conditions. In all seven study reaches, the dams had the effect of decreasing annual high flows. For the North Santiam River Reaches 1, 2, and 3, the median of annual 1-day maximum streamflows decreased 42, 50, and 50 percent, respectively, under regulated streamflow conditions. Likewise in the South Santiam River basin, the median of annual 1-day maximum streamflows for Reaches 4, 5, and 6 decreased 39, 52, and 51 percent, respectively. In contrast to their effect on high flows, the dams had the effect of increasing low flows. The median of annual 7-day minimum flows in six of the seven study reaches increased under regulated streamflow conditions from 25 to 334 percent depending on the reach. On a seasonal basis, median monthly streamflows decreased from February to May and increased from September to January in all the reaches. However, the magnitude of these changes usually decreased in the reaches farther downstream from dams because of natural tributary and groundwater inflow entering the river below the dams. At the North Santiam River at Mehama gage, bankfull discharge was exceeded on average 3.39 times per year prior to construction of the dams in 1953. After the dams were built, bankfull discharge has been exceeded on average only 0.97 times per year. Farther downstream from the dams at the Santiam River at Jefferson gage, bankfull discharge was exceeded on average 7.46 times per year prior to the construction of the dams in 1953. After the dams were built, bankfull discharge has been exceeded, on average, 4.12 times per year. Climatic differences between the pre- and post-dam periods also were assessed in the study. A Wilcox rank-sum test of monthly precipitation data from Salem and Waterloo found no significant difference between the two periods. That would suggest that the operation of the dams since the 1950s and 1960s is the primary cause of alterations to the Santiam River basin streamflow regime.

The geomorphology and the possible geomorphic and ecological changes in response to river-flow modifications were characterized. The characterization was based primarily on qualitative observations and information from previous studies. Channel processes, including meander migration, bar growth, and creation and maintenance of secondary channel features, are mainly determined by the flow and coarse-sediment regimes; however, these processes have been altered by flow releases from the upstream dams.

The North Santiam River below Big Cliff Dam transitions from a narrow channel confined by steep bedrock valley walls to a broad, alluvial river with many side channels and gravel bars before joining the South Santiam River near Jefferson. Overall, there is little revetment along the North Santiam study reaches.

The South Santiam River below Foster Dam occupies mostly a low-sinuosity, single-thread channel with a flood plain. Active gravel bars are sparse and small (less than 1,500 yd^2). Instead, the reach has a number of densely vegetated bar surfaces relict of gravel bars that were active before dam and revetment construction. Much of the reach presently is stabilized by revetments constructed in the mid- to late 20th century. Bank stabilization, in combination with construction of the Foster and Big Cliff Dams, resulted in substantial reductions in channel complexity.

The main-stem Santiam River below the confluence of the North and South Santiam Rivers historically had dynamic, multi-thread channels that were prone to rapid meander migration and avulsion prior to flood control and bank protection. The reach flows through a broad flood plain that ranges up to 3 mi wide. However, bank revetment currently flanks much of the channel, restricting bank erosion, channel complexity, and bar growth. Many relict bar surfaces and secondary channel features presently have dense vegetative cover.

Historically, the Santiam River basin supported diverse aquatic and terrestrial ecosystems ranging from steep, pool-riffle channel systems, abundant large wood, and riparian forests dominated by upland species in the upper reaches to dynamic multi-thread channels containing off-channel and secondary features, with alder and cottonwood forests flanking and interacting with the channel in the lower reaches and main stem. Similar to the Middle and Coast Fork Willamette and McKenzie River basins, many of these habitats have been substantially altered by modifications in the river flow and sediment regimes or are inaccessible because of passage issues at dams. The streamflow analysis and geomorphic characterization provide a framework to develop environmental flows to restore the historic diverse aquatic and terrestrial ecosystems.

Suggestions for future ecological monitoring and investigations in the Santiam River basin include additional streamflow data collection and analysis, computing bed-material transport rates and a sediment budget, a detailed channel and flood-plain morphology assessment, and determining terrestrial and aquatic responses to streamflow management.

Acknowledgements

The authors thank Christine Budai, Keith Duffy, Jerry Otto, and Greg Taylor, Portland District, U.S. Army Corps of Engineers; Leslie Bach, The Nature Conservancy, Portland, Oregon; Mike McCord and Michael Mattick, Oregon Water Resources Department; and Jay Spillum, U.S. Geological Survey Oregon Water Science Center for their assistance in this study.

References Cited

Acreman, M., and Dunbar, M.J., 2004, Defining environmental flow requirements–A review: Hydrology and Earth System Sciences, v. 8, no. 5, p. 861–876.

Bragg, H.M., Sobieszczyk, Steven, Uhrich, M.A., and Piatt, D.R., 2007, Suspended-sediment loads and yields in the North Santiam River basin, Oregon, water years 1999-2004: U.S. Geological Survey Scientific Investigations Report 2007–5187, 27 p.

Bragg, H.M., and Uhrich, M.A., 2010, Suspended-sediment budget for the North Santiam River basin, Oregon, water years 2005–08: U.S. Geological Survey Scientific Investigations Report 2010–5038, 26 p.

Buccola, N.L., and Rounds, S.A., 2011, Simulating potential structural and operational changes for Detroit Dam on the North Santiam River, Oregon—Interim Results: U.S. Geological Survey Open-File Report 2011–1268, 25 p.

Conlon, T.D., Wozniak, K.C., Woodcock, Douglas, Herrera, N.B., Fisher, B.J., Morgan, D.S.,

Lee, K.K., and Hinkle, S.R., 2005, Groundwater hydrology of the Willamette basin, Oregon: U.S. Geological Survey Scientific Investigations Report 2005–5168, 83 p.

Cooper, R.M., 2002, Determining surface water availability in Oregon: State of Oregon Water Resources Department Open-File Report SW 02–002, 157 p.

E and S Environmental Chemistry, Inc., 2002, North Santiam River watershed assessment: Corvallis, Oregon, 290 p., accessed July 2, 2012, at *http://www.nsantiamwatershed.org/wp-content /uploads/2009/09/NSW_Assessment.pdf.*

E and S Environmental Chemistry, Inc., and South Santiam Watershed Council, 2000, South Santiam watershed assessment: Corvallis, Oregon, 224 p., accessed July 2, 2012, at *http://www.sswc.org/wp-content/uploads/2008/12/South-Santiam-Watershed-Assessment-January-2000.pdf.*

Fletcher, W.B., and Davidson, L.D., 1988, South Santiam River Bank Protection Study, Pilot Project for Willamette River Bank Protection Study: Portland, Oregon, U.S. Army Corps of Engineers, 36 p.

Gregory, S., Ashkenas, L., Haggerty, P., Oetter, D., Wildman, K., Hulse, D., Branscomb, A. and Van Sickle, J., 2002a, Riparian vegetation, *in* Hulse, D., Gregory, S., and Baker, J., eds., Willamette River basin atlas: Corvallis, Oregon, Oregon State University Press, p. 40., accessed July 2, 2012, at *http://www.fsl.orst.edu/pnwerc/wrb/Atlas_web_ compressed/4.Biotic_Systems/4c.riparian_ veg_web.pdf.*

Gregory, S., Ashkenas, L., Oetter, D., Minear, P. and Wildman, K., 2002b, Historical Willamette River channel change, *in* Hulse, D., Gregory, S., and Baker, J., eds., Willamette River basin atlas: Corvallis, Oregon, Oregon State University Press, p. 18–24., accessed July 2, 2012, at *http://www.fsl.orst.edu/pnwerc/wrb/ Atlas_web_compressed/ 3.Water_Resources/3c.historic_chl_web.pdf.*

Gregory, S., Ashkenas, L., and Nygaard, C., 2007a, Summary report to assist development of ecosystem flow recommendations for the Middle Fork and Coast Fork of the Willamette River, Oregon: Corvallis, Oregon, Institute for Water and Watersheds, Oregon State University, 237 p.

Gregory, S., Ashkenas, L., and Nygaard, C., 2007b, Summary report—Environmental flows workshop for the Middle Fork and Coast Fork of the Willamette River, Oregon: Corvallis, Oregon, Institute for Water and Watersheds, Oregon State University, 34 p.

Hansen, R.P., and Crumrine, M.D., 1991, The effects of multipurpose reservoirs on the water temperature of the North and South Santiam Rivers, Oregon: U.S. Geological Survey Water Resources Investigation Report 91–4007, 51 p.

Helm, D.C., and Leonard, A.R., 1977, Ground-water resources of the lower Santiam River basin, middle Willamette Valley, Oregon: Oregon Water Resources Department--Groundwater Reports, vii, 75 p.

Hill, B.E., and Priest, G.R., 1992, Geologic setting of the Santiam Pass area, central Cascade Range, Oregon: State of Oregon, Department of Geology and Mineral Industries Open-File Report, O-92-3, pp. 5–18

Interagency Committee on Water Data, 1982, Guidelines for determining flood flow frequency—Bulletin #17B of the Hydrology Subcommittee: Reston, Virginia, U.S. Geological Survey, accessed April 27, 2012, at *http://water.usgs.gov/osw/bulletin17b/dl_flow.pdf*.

Klingeman, P.C., 1973, Indications of streambed degradation in the Willamette Valley: Corvallis, Oregon, Oregon State University, Water Resources Research Institute Report WRRI–21, 99 p.

Laenen, Antonius, and Risley, J.C., 1997, Precipitation-runoff and streamflow-routing models for the Willamette River basin, Oregon: U.S. Geological Survey Water-Resources Investigations Report 95–4284, 197 p.

Laenen, Antonius, and Hansen, R.P., 1985, Preliminary study of the water-temperature regime of the North Santiam River downstream from Detroit and Big Cliff Dams, Oregon: U.S. Geological Survey Water Resources Investigation Report 84–4105, 45 p.

Lee, K.K., and Risley, J.C., 2002, Estimates of ground-water recharge, base flow, and stream reach gains and losses in the Willamette River basin, Oregon: U.S. Geological Survey Water-Resources Investigations Report 01–4215, 52 p.

National Marine Fisheries Service, 2008a, Endangered Species Act Status of West Coast Salmon and Steelhead: , Seattle, Washington, NOAA National Marine Fisheries Service, Northwest Region, accessed May 22, 2012, at *http://www.nwr.noaa.gov/ESA-Salmon-Listings/upload/1-pgr-8-11.pdf.90*

National Marine Fisheries Service, 2008b, Endangered Species Act Section 7(a)(2) Consultation biological opinion and Magnuson-Stevens fishery conservation and management act essential fish habitat consultation: Seattle, Washington, NOAA National Marine Fisheries Service, Northwest Region, NOAA Fisheries Log Number FINWRl2000/02117, [various pagination], accessed January 16, 2012, at *http://www.nwr.noaa.gov/Salmon-Hydropower/Willamette-basin/Willamette-BO.cfm*.

O'Connor, J.E., Sarna-Wojcicki, Andrei, Wozniak, K.C., Polette, D.J., and Fleck, R.J., 2001, Origin, extent, and thickness of Quaternary geologic units in Willamette Valley, Oregon: U.S. Geological Survey Professional Paper 1620, 52 p. Dataset available online at *http://or.water.usgs.gov/pubs_dir/Online/Cd/WRIR99-4036/GIS_FILES/will_geol.html*, accessed January 11, 2012.

Oregon Department of Environmental Quality, 2006, Willamette basin total maximum daily load order memorandum: accessed November 30, 2011, at *http://www.deq.state.or.us/wq/tmdls/docs/willamettebasin/willamette/ordermemo.pdf*.

Oregon Water Resources Department, 2012, Water use reporting database: accessed March 7, 2012, at *http://apps.wrd.state.or.us/apps/wr/wateruse_report/*.

Piatt, D.R., Johnston, M.W., Bragg, H.M., Brooks, A.M., Sobieszczyk, Steven, and Uhrich, M.A., 2011, Water-quality in the North Santiam River basin, Oregon—Comparison of water-quality data for water year 2007 with the preceding period of record: U.S. Geological Survey Open-File Report 2011–1008, 75 p.

Reiser, D.W., and White, R.G., 1983, Effects of complete redd dewatering on salmonid egg-hatching success and development of juveniles: Transactions of American Fisheries Society, v. 112, p. 532–540.

Richter, B.D., Warner, A.T., Meyer, J.L., and Lutz, K., 2006, A collaborative and adaptive process for developing environmental flow recommendations: River Research and Applications, v. 22, p. 297–318, DOI: 10.1002/rra.892.

Risley, John, Wallick, J.R., Waite, Ian, and Stonewall, Adam, 2010a, Development of an environmental flow framework for the McKenzie River basin, Oregon: U.S. Geological Survey Scientific Investigations Report 2010–5016, 94 p.

Risley, J.C., Bach, L., and Wallick, J.R., 2010b, Summary report—Environmental flows workshop for the McKenzie River, Oregon: The Nature Conservancy, Portland, Oregon, 40 p.

Rounds, S.A., 2010, Thermal effects of dams in the Willamette River basin, Oregon: U.S. Geological Survey Scientific Investigations Report 2010–5153, 64 p.

Sherrod, D., Ingebritsen, S.E., Curless, J.M., Keith, T.E., Diaz, N.M., and DeRoo, T.G., and Hurlocker, S.L., 1996, Water, rocks, and woods; a field excursion to examine the geology, hydrology, and geothermal resources in the Clackamas, North Santiam, and McKenzie River drainages, Cascade Range, Oregon: Oregon Geology, v. 58, no. 5, 103 p.

Sobieszczyk, Steven, Uhrich, M.A., and Bragg, H.M., 2007, Major turbidity events in the North Santiam River basin, Oregon, water years 1999–2004: U.S. Geological Survey Scientific Investigations Report 2007–5178, 51 p.

Speers, D.D., and Versteeg, J.D., 1982, Runoff forecasting for reservoir operations—The past and the future (Santiam River basin, Detroit reservoir), Proceedings of the Eastern Snow Conference, 39th annual meeting, April 19–23, Reno, Nevada: p. 149–156.

Sullivan, A.B., and Rounds, S.A., 2004, Modeling streamflow and water temperature in the North Santiam and Santiam Rivers, Oregon, 2001–02: U.S. Geological Survey Scientific Investigations Report 2004–5001, 36 p.

Sullivan, A.B., Rounds, S.A., Sobieszczyk, Steven, and Bragg, H.M., 2007, Modeling hydrodynamics, water temperature, and suspended sediment in Detroit Lake, Oregon: U.S. Geological Survey Scientific Investigations Report 2007–5008, 40 p.

Tharme, R.E., 2003, A global perspective on environmental flow assessment: emerging trends in the development and application of environmental flow methodologies for rivers: River Research and Applications, v. 19, p. 397–441, DOI: 10.1002/rra.736.

Thayer, T.P., 1936, Geology of the Salem Hills and the North Santiam River basin, Oregon: Oregon Department of Geology and Mineral Industries, Bulletin no. 15, 40 p.

Thayer, T.P., 1936, Structure of the North Santiam River section of the Cascade Mountains in Oregon: The Journal of Geology, v. 44, no. 6, p. 701–716.

The Nature Conservancy, 2007, Indicators of hydrologic alteration—Version 7 User's manual: The Nature Conservancy, 75 p., accessed December 19, 2011, at *http://conserveonline.org/workspaces/iha/documents/download/view.html*.

The Nature Conservancy, 2009, The Sustainable Rivers Project: accessed November 18, 2011, at http://www.nature.org/ourinitiatives/habitats/riverslakes/sustainable-rivers-project.xml

Uhrich, M.A., and Bragg, H.M., 2003, Monitoring instream turbidity to estimate continuous suspended-sediment loads and yields and clay-water volumes in the Upper North Santiam River basin, Oregon, 1998–2000: U.S. Geological Survey Water Resources Investigation Report 03–4098, 44 p.

U.S. Army Corps of Engineers (USACE), 2007, Supplemental biological assessment of the effects of the Willamette River basin flood control project on species listed under the Endangered Species Act—Submitted to National Marine Fisheries Service and U.S. Fish and Wildlife Service, [variously paged]: accessed May 22, 2012, at http://www.nwp.usace.army.mil/Portals/24/docs/environment/biop/Final_Will_Suppl_BA.pdf

U.S. Fish and Wildlife Service (USFWS), 2008, Final Biological Opinion on the continued operation and maintenance of the Willamette River basin Project and effects to Oregon Chub, Bull Trout, and Bull Trout Critical Habitat designated under the Endangered Species Act—Submitted to U.S. Army Corps of Engineers, Bonneville Power Administration, and Bureau of Reclamation, [variously paged]: accessed January 16, 2012, at http://www.nwr.noaa.gov/Salmon-Hydropower/Willamette-basin/Willamette-BO.cfm.

U.S. Geological Survey, 2012, StreamStats: accessed March 7, 2012, at http://water.usgs.gov/osw/streamstats/index.html.

Wallick, J.R., Lancaster, S.T., and Bolte, J.P., 2006, Determination of bank erodibility for natural and anthropogenic bank materials using a model of lateral migration and observed erosion along the Willamette River, Oregon—USA: River Research and Applications, v. 22, p. 631–649.

Wallick, J.R., Grant, G.E., Lancaster, S.T., Bolte, J.P., and Denlinger, R.P., 2007, Patterns and controls on historical channel change in the Willamette River, Oregon, in Gupta, A.V., ed., Large rivers—Geomorphology and management: John Wiley and Sons, p. 491–516.

Wallick, J.R., Anderson, S.W., Cannon, Charles, and O'Connor, J.E., 2010, Channel change and bed-material transport in the lower Chetco River, Oregon: U.S. Geological Survey Scientific Investigations Report 2010–5065, 68 p.

Wallick, J.R., O'Connor, J.E., Anderson, Scott, Keith, Mackenzie, Cannon, Charles, and Risley, J.C., 2011, Channel change and bed-material transport in the Umpqua River basin, Oregon: U.S. Geological Survey Scientific Investigations Report 2011–5041, 112 p., accessed November 10, 2011, at http://pubs.usgs.gov/sir/2011/5041/.

Western Regional Climate Center, 2012, Website—Cooperative climatological data summaries: accessed June 14, 2012, at http://www.wrcc.dri.edu/climatedata/climsum/.

Wolman, M.G., and Miller, J.P., 1960, Magnitude and frequency of forces in geomorphic processes: Journal of Geology, v. 68, no. 1, p. 54–74.

Appendix A. Streamflow Data Time-Series Extension

Microsoft® Excel® files containing the daily mean streamflow data time-series extensions for each of the seven study reaches can be downloaded from *http://pubs.usgs.gov/of/2012/1133/*.

In each file, there is a "Read me" worksheet that explains how the streamflow time series for the reach was extended to cover missing periods. Each file also includes computed unregulated daily-mean streamflow data time series, provided by the U.S. Army Corps of Engineers, which were used in the study. The equations used to compute the unregulated daily-mean streamflow time series are provided in Appendix B.

Appendix B. U.S. Army Corps of Engineers Computed Unregulated Streamflow Data Time Series

This appendix contains methods and equations from U.S. Army Corps of Engineers used to compute six daily mean unregulated streamflow time series for the Santiam River basin (Keith Duffy, U.S. Army Corps of Engineers, written commun., 2011). One or more of these six time series were used in each of the seven Excel files described in Appendix A. However, all six time series are shown together in the worksheet labeled "2. Unregulated flow" in the Flow_extension_reach7.xls Excel file.

1. North Santiam River at Detroit Dam

10/01/1935–09/30/1938

Combined observed flows of:

USGS 14178000 (North Santiam River above Boulder Creek near Detroit, Oregon) and

USGS 14179000 (Breitenbush River above French Creek near Detroit, Oregon)

Plus local inflows computed as:

USGS 14183000 (North Santiam River at Mehama, Oregon)

Minus the sum of:

USGS 14182500 (Little North Santiam River near Mehama, Oregon),

USGS 14178000 (lagged by 6 hours), and

USGS 14179000 (lagged by 6 hours)

Adjusted by a drainage area ratio (DAR) of 0.509

10/01/1938–10/30/1952

Observed flow of:

USGS 14181500 (North Santiam River at Niagara, Oregon)

Adjusted by DAR (0.960)

10/01/1952–09/30/1960

   Calculated inflow (Modified Flows)

   Adjusted by DAR (0.960)

10/01/1960–09/30/2009

   Quality controlled Dataquery project inflows

2. Local inflows to North Santiam River at Mehama, Oregon (14183000)

10/01/1935–09/30/1938

   Observed flow of:

      USGS 14172500 (Little North Santiam River near Mehama, Oregon)

   Plus local inflows computed as:

      USGS 14183000 (North Santiam River at Mehama, Oregon)

   Minus the sum of:

      USGS 14182500 (Little North Santiam River near Mehama, Oregon),

      USGS 14178000 (lagged by 6 hours), and

      USGS 14179000 (lagged by 6 hours)

   Adjusted by DAR (0.491)

10/01/1938–09/30/2009

   Observed flow of:

      USGS 14183000 (North Santiam River at Mehama, Oregon)

   Minus routed flow of:

      USGS 14181500 (North Santiam River at Niagara, Oregon)

   Adjusted by DAR (1.091)

3. Middle Santiam River at Green Peter Dam

10/01/1935–09/30/1947

   Observed flow of:

      USGS 14186000 (Middle Santiam River near Foster, Oregon)

10/01/1947–09/30/1950

Observed flow of:

USGS 14185000 (South Santiam River below Cascadia, Oregon)

Adjusted by regression coefficient (2.022)

10/01/1950–09/30/1966

Observed flow of:

USGS 14186500 (Middle Santiam River at mouth near Foster, Oregon)

Adjusted by DAR (0.959)

10/01/1966–06/21/1967

Combined observed flow of:

USGS 14185800 (Middle Santiam River near Cascadia, Oregon) and

USGS 14185900 (Quartzville Creek near Cascadia, Oregon)

Sum adjusted by regression coefficient (1.245)

06/22/1967–09/30/2009

Calculated inflow (Dataquery)

4. Local inflows to South Santiam River at Foster Dam

10/1/1935–8/22/1968

Observed flow of:

USGS 14185000 (South Santiam River below Cascadia, Oregon)

Adjusted by regression coefficient (1.194)

8/23/1968–9/30/2009

Calculated inflow (Dataquery) minus Green Peter outflow (Dataquery)

5. Local inflows to South Santiam River at Waterloo, Oregon (14187500)

10/01/1935–09/30/1947

Observed flow of:

USGS 14187500 (South Santiam River at Waterloo, Oregon)

Minus combined routed flow of:

    USGS 14185000 (South Santiam River below Cascadia, Oregon) and

    USGS 14186000 (Middle Santiam River near Foster, Oregon)

Adjusted by DAR (0.761)

10/01/1947–09/30/1950

    Observed flow of:

        USGS 14187500 (South Santiam River at Waterloo, Oregon)

    Minus routed flow of:

        USGS 14185000 (South Santiam River below Cascadia, Oregon)

    Adjusted by DAR (0.318)

10/01/1950–09/30/1966

    Observed flow of:

        USGS 14187500 (South Santiam River at Waterloo, Oregon)

    Minus combined routed flow of:

        USGS 14185000 (South Santiam River below Cascadia, Oregon) and

        USGS 14186500 (Middle Santiam River at mouth near Foster, Oregon)

    Adjusted by DAR (0.829)

10/01/1966–07/31/1973

    Observed flow of:

        USGS 14187500 (South Santiam River at Waterloo, Oregon)

    Minus routed flow of:

        USGS 14186700 (South Santiam River at Foster, Oregon)

08/01/1973–09/29/1988

    Observed flow of:

        USGS 14187500 (South Santiam River at Waterloo, Oregon)

    Minus routed flow of:

        USGS 14187200 (South Santiam River near Foster, Oregon)

    Adjusted by DAR (1.037)

    Plus routed flow of:

        USGS 14187100 (Wiley Creek at Foster, Oregon)

09/30/1988 -09/30/2009

    Observed flow of:

        USGS 14187500 (South Santiam River at Waterloo, Oregon)

    Minus routed flow of:

        USGS 14187200 (South Santiam River near Foster, Oregon)

    Adjusted by DAR (1.164)

    Plus routed flow of:

        USGS 14187000 (Wiley Creek near Foster, Oregon)

6. Local inflows to Santiam River at Jefferson, Oregon (14189000)

10/01/1935–09/30/1939

    Observed flow of:

        USGS 14191000 (Willamette River at Salem, Oregon)

    Minus combined routed flows of:

        USGS 14187500 (South Santiam River at Waterloo, Oregon),

        USGS 14183000 (North Santiam River at Mehama, Oregon), and

        USGS 14174000 (Willamette River at Albany, Oregon)

    Adjusted by DAR (0.433)

10/01/1939–09/30/2009

    Observed flow of:

        USGS 14189000 (Santiam River at Jefferson, Oregon)

    Minus combined routed flows of:

        USGS 14187500 (South Santiam River at Waterloo, Oregon)

        USGS 14183000 (North Santiam River at Mehama, Oregon)

Appendix C. Indicators of Hydrologic Alteration Results

Microsoft Excel files containing the results of the Indicator of Hydrologic Alteration analysis for each of the seven study reaches may be downloaded from *http://pubs.usgs.gov/of/2012/1133/*.

Appendix D. Description of Study Reaches

A Microsoft Excel spreadsheet containing descriptions of the seven study reaches may be accessed at *http://pubs.usgs.gov/of/2012/1133/*.